TEMPO

Chris Barker
Libby Mitchell

1

Student's Book

MACMILLAN

G000320732

Communication Pronunciation	Skills Culture Spot Portfolio	Workbook Study tips
Saying hello and goodbye Classroom language: *How do you say ... in English?* Talking about your family: *This is my sister.*		Vocabulary practice WB (Workbook) ex. 1–7 Grammar practice WB ex. 8–19
Introducing yourself: *Hello. I'm Mrs Wilson.* Talking about nationality: *I'm Spanish.* *Hello./Hi.* *Welcome!* *Come in.* *Goodbye.* *Thank you./Thanks.* *See you tomorrow.* *Good morning.* Words which rhyme: *you, blue*	Schools in Britain Write about a favourite sports star, film star or band Write about yourself WB p.17	SB p. 17 ⟶ WB ex. 1–2 SB pp. 20–1 WB ex. 3–8 SB pp. 22–3 WB ex. 9–13 SB pp. 26–7 WB pp. 16–17
Asking and talking about family and possessions: *I've got a sister. Have you got your pencil case?* Talking about school subjects and the school timetable: *What have we got on Friday afternoon?* *See you later!* *He's lucky!* *OK.* *She's really cute!* *Really?* /h/	International e-pals: giving personal information Find out and write about a famous person	SB p. 29 ⟶ WB ex. 1–2 SB pp. 30–4 WB ex. 3–12 SB pp. 36–7 WB pp. 26–7 How to remember vocabulary WB ex. 4 p. 27
Describing rooms and furniture: *My room's quite small. There's a bed.* *Oh yes.* *What?* *Look at this.* *Yuck!* *It's great!* /ʌ/	From a tree house to the White House Design and label your ideal house Write a description of your bedroom WB p. 39	SB p. 41 ⟶ WB ex.1–2 SB pp. 42–3 WB ex.4–7 SB pp. 44–5 WB ex. 8–11 SB p. 46 WB ex. 12–13 SB pp. 48–9 WB pp. 38–9
Asking permission and talking about possibility: *Can I go karting? Perhaps we can go for a pizza.* Asking and saying the time: *It's quarter to two.* *Perhaps we can go to the cinema.* *Thanks a lot!* *How are you?* *I'm fine, thanks.* *Oh, never mind.* *I'm sorry I can't come to your party.* *Surprise, surprise!* *Happy birthday!* /æ/ or /ɑː/	Birthdays Write a birthday message	SB p. 51 ⟶ WB ex. 1–2 SB pp. 52–5 WB ex. 3–10 SB p. 56 WB ex. 11 SB pp. 58–9 WB pp. 48–9 Organising vocabulary in charts WB ex. 4 p. 49

Communication Pronunciation	Skills Culture Spot Portfolio	Workbook Study tips
Talking about free-time activities and holidays: *I read. I go out with my friends.* *Thanks for your help.* *You're welcome!* *Sure, no problem.* *You bet!* Third person Present simple endings /s/ /z/ /ɪz/	School holidays: activity centres Write an interview for a magazine Write about your holidays WB p. 61	SB p. 63 ⟶ WB ex. 1–2 SB pp. 64–7 WB ex. 3–11, 13 SB p. 68 WB ex. 12, 14 SB pp. 70–1 WB pp. 60–1
Talking about daily activities: *I get up at ...* Talking about frequency: *I usually walk to school.* *Test? What test?* *You're in trouble!* *Well, let's see.* *What's the matter?* *That's easy.* /ɪ/ /iː/	Survey: all about you Ask your favourite star about his/her daily activities	SB p. 73 ⟶ WB ex. 1 SB pp. 74–5 WB ex. 2–8 SB pp. 76–7 WB ex. 9–10 SB pp. 80–1 WB pp. 70–1 Organising grammar in charts WB ex. 2 p. 70
Talking about ability: *Can you dance?* Talking about feelings and states: *I'm hot.* *Of course.* *You know.* *Not really.* *That's fine.* *Watch this.* /ð/ /θ/	What do you like about Britain? Make up an animal quiz Write about your abilities WB p. 83	SB p. 85 ⟶ WB ex. 1–2 SB pp. 86–9 WB ex. 4–11 SB p. 90 WB ex. 3 SB pp. 92–3 WB pp. 82–3
Giving instructions: *Sit down.* Talking about places in a town: *There's a leisure centre.* Describing the position of objects and places: *It's next to ...* *This is important.* *Just a minute.* *What else?* *Right.* *Be careful!* Stressed syllables	Days out: information about what there is to do in Manchester and London Create an information sheet about a town	SB p. 95 ⟶ WB ex. 1 SB p. 96 WB ex. 2–7 SB p. 97 WB ex. 8 SB pp. 98–100 WB ex. 9 Keeping vocabulary records WB ex. 3 p. 92 SB pp. 102–3 WB pp. 92–3
Describing people and clothes: *She's quite tall. She's got long brown hair.* Talking about present actions: *Are you doing your homework?* *It's time for school.* *Poor thing.* *I'm in a bad mood.* *What's up?* *It's only (a football match).* *Don't worry about it.* /ŋ/	Our trip to London: things to see and do in London Design a clothes catalogue page or describe a holiday photo Write information about your town for a tourist WB p. 105	SB p. 107 ⟶ WB ex. 1 SB pp. 108–9 WB ex. 3–8 SB pp. 110–11 WB ex. 9–11 SB pp. 114–15 WB pp. 104–5
Talking on the phone: *Hello, is that Nick? It's Ricky here.* Describing what you're doing: *I'm calling from the plane.* Comparing what you usually do with what you're doing at the moment: *Lucky thing!* *Wow!* *What about you?* *Lovely!* *Disgusting!* *Mmm.* *Sounds great!* *Have a great time!* *See you in September.* /ʌ/ /æ/	Families around the world: daily routines and cultural differences. Find some simple recipes on the internet	SB p. 117 ⟶ WB ex. 1 SB pp. 118–19 WB ex. 3–8 SB pp. 120–2 WB ex. 9 SB pp. 124–5 WB pp. 114–15 Finding the meaning of unknown vocabulary WB ex. 4–5 p.115

Portfolio pages 129 –135

Page 136 Word list

Welcome!
Introducing yourself

- Possessive adjective *my*
- Personal pronouns: *I, you, he, she*
- Saying hello and goodbye
- Present simple of *be*, affirmative, singular

🎧 Listen

1 **Listen and read.**

Grammar focus

Present simple of *be*: affirmative, singular
Read the dialogue above, then write the short forms here.

Long form	Short form
I am (Charlie.)	I'm...
You are	You......
He is	He......
She is	She......
It is	It's.....

🎧 Listen

2 **Complete the sentences.**

1 Hello! ...I'm... Sam.
2 This .... Anna.
3 .... my sister.
4 This .... Sam.

5 .... my brother.
6 Hello. .... Kate.
7 .... my friend.

🎧 Listen

3 **Listen and repeat.**

4 **Talk with your classmates.**

A Hello, I'm Eleanor. This is Julia. She's my friend.

B Hi, I'm John. This is Mark. He's my friend.

5 **Listen and read.** 🎧

Speak

6 **Practise the dialogue.**

Write

7 **Complete the phrases.**

1

2

3

4

0

Classroom language

Read

1 **How do you say these things in your language?**

a Please, Miss!

b I don't understand. Can you repeat that, please?

c What does 'favourite' mean?

d How do you say 🚽 in English?

e How do you spell 'English'? THIS IS MY...BOOK

f Sorry I'm late.

Listen and write

2 **Listen and write the letters.** 1 ....f....

Listen and read

3 **Listen to the teacher and mime the actions.**

1 Open your books at page eight.

2 Listen to the cassette.

3 Read the dialogue.

4 Write the answers.

5 Work with your partner.

6 Look at the board.

7 Put your hand up.

Vocabulary

(4) Write the words.

book   computer

clock   bag   pen

chair

paper   window

pencil

blackboard   door   ruler

teacher

rubber

desk

1 ....

2 ....

3 ....

4 ....

5 ....

6 ....

7 ....

8 ....

9 ....

10 ....

11 ....

12 ....

13 ....

14 ....

15 ....

Remember! You add an 's' to form the regular plural of words.

book – books   pen – pens

The alphabet

Days of the week

🎧 Listen and read

1 Listen and repeat.

ABCDEFGHIJKLMNOPQRSTUVWXYZ
abcdefghijklmnopqrstuvwxyz

2 Now listen to the song. Can you sing it?

ABCD
EFGH
IJKL
MN
OPQR
STUV
WXY
Z

🎧 Listen and write

3a Listen and write the letters.

1 ....GB........   4 ....

2 ....   5 ....

3 ....

3b What do the letters stand for?

1 ....GB.......... Great Britain.........................

4 Work with a partner. Guess which American states the letters stand for.

1 CO   ....Colorado....................................
2 CA   ....
3 NY   ....
4 NJ   ....
5 FL   ....
6 TX   ....
7 OK   ....
8 WA   ....

5 Listen and complete the sentence.

My name's Wallace. And this is my dog ....

Speak

6 Ask and answer questions.

A How do you spell your name?

B ....

10

Days of the week

Write

7a Write the days of the week in the correct order.

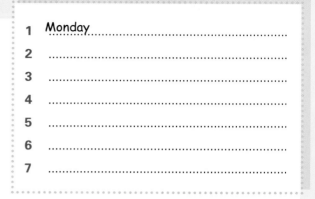

1 Monday ....
2 ....
3 ....
4 ....
5 ....
6 ....
7 ....

Tuesday
Saturday
Wednesday
Monday
Sunday
Friday
Thursday

Days of the week always start
with a capital letter.

Speak

7b Work with a partner. Spell the days of
the week. Take turns to say each letter.

Partner A: (M)

Partner B: (O)

Partner A: (N)

8 Complete the grid with the days of the week.

				O	

R

U

0

Numbers and colours

- Numbers: 0 – 20
- Question words: *What? How?*
- Colours

Listen and write

1 Listen and repeat.

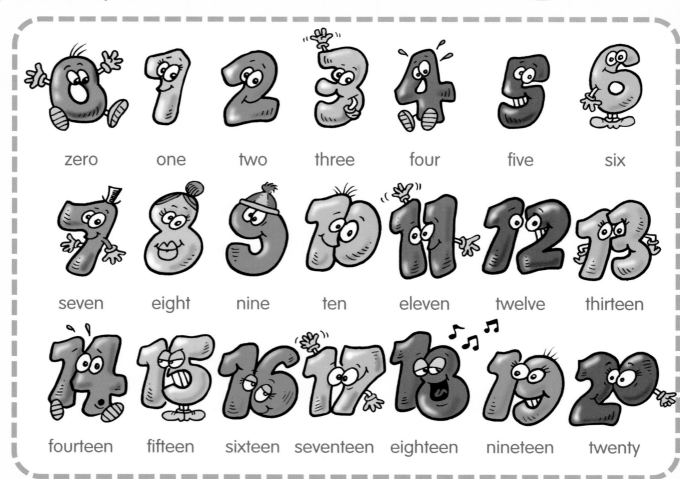

| zero | one | two | three | four | five | six |

| seven | eight | nine | ten | eleven | twelve | thirteen |

| fourteen | fifteen | sixteen | seventeen | eighteen | nineteen | twenty |

2 Listen and write the ages.

1 13........................
2 ....
3 ....
4 ....
5 ....
6 ....
7 ....
8 ....
9 ....
10 ....

3 Listen and write the numbers.

1 1, 2 ....
2 ....
3 ....

4 Work with a partner. One person says six numbers and the other person writes them down. Change roles.

Speak

5a Ask and answer questions.

A How old are you?

B ....

5b Who's got brothers and sisters? Ask and answer questions.

A How old is your brother?

B He's seventeen.

A How old is your sister?

B She's three.

12

Listen and read

6 **Listen to the colours.**

blue

green

yellow

white

black

red

orange

purple

brown

pink

grey

Listen and write

7 **Listen and write the colours.**

1 yellow..........   3 ....   5 ....

2 ....   4 ....

Speak

8 **Ask and answer questions.**

> A What's your favourite colour?

> B My favourite colour's ......

Read and listen

9a **Can you guess the missing words?**

My name's Sue.
My favourite colour's ..blue..
My favourite number's ....
How are ....?

My name's Faye
My favourite colour's ....
My dog is Jay.
And I'm ....

9b **Now listen and check.**

0

Talking about your family

- Present simple of *be*, affirmative, plural
- Personal pronouns: *we, you, they*
- Members of the family
- Question word: *Who?*
- *a* and *an*

Listen and read

1 Listen and find the people in the photo.

Nicola	This is my family. This is me.
Justin	Oh, yes!
Nicola	This is my brother, Ben, and this is my sister, Claire.
Justin	Mmm.
Nicola	This is my mother and this is my father. This is Liz and this is Mike. They're my aunt and uncle.
Justin	Oh, yes.
Nicola	And this is Daniel.
Justin	Who's Daniel?
Nicola	He's my cousin. We're the same age. We're both eleven.
Justin	And who are they?
Nicola	They're my grandparents. They're great!

Sue: **my grandmother**

Mike: **my uncle**

Richard: **my grandfather**

Liz: **my aunt**

Paul: **my father**

Claire: **my sister**

Ben: **my brother**

Nicola: **me**

Hayley: **my mother**

Daniel: **my cousin**

mother and father = parents
grandmother and grandfather = grandparents

Grammar focus

Present simple of *be*: affirmative, plural

Look at what Nicola says about her family. Complete the table.

Long form	Short form
We are (eleven.)	We......
You are	You.'re.
They are	They......

Listen and write

2 Listen and complete the sentences.

1 We're .... the same age.
2 .... my grandparents.
3 .... great!
4 .... eleven.
5 .... my aunt and uncle.
6 .... great!

Speak

3 Write the names of members of your family. Then ask and answer questions.

Sylvia, Richard, Angela, Mark

A Who's Sylvia?

B She's my grandmother.

Write

4 Write the names of members of your family. Explain their relationship to you.

1 Sylvia, my grandmother
2 ....
3 ....
4 ....
5 ....
6 ....

Listen and write

5 Listen and write *a* or *an*.

1 ..a.. book

2 ..an.. apple

3 ...... cat

4 ...... dog

5 ...... girl

6 ...... boy

7 ...... egg

8 ...... ice cream

9 ...... banana

10 ...... orange

11 ...... umbrella

12 .... bike

Use *a* before a word starting with a consonant and *an* before a word starting with a vowel.

Vocabulary

6 Look at the pictures for 20 seconds. Now close your book. How many things can you remember?

Are you ready?

1 Choose the correct words to complete the sentences.

Claudia and I ..are. ten.

A is   **B** am   **C** are

1 Hello! ....'m Carl.

    A You   **B** I   **C** He

2 This is Sara. .... my sister.

    A He's   **B** It's   **C** She's

3 Robert and Frank .... my brothers.

    A is   **B** are   **C** am

4 Good morning! How .... you?

    A are   **B** is   **C** am

5 This is Kevin. .... my brother.

    A We're   **B** She's   **C** He's

2 Write the missing words.

Monday, ...Tuesday...., Wednesday,
Thursday, ..., Saturday,
....

3 Write the numbers.

    seventeen   .17..   **4** twenty   ......

1 eleven   ......   **5** fifteen   ......

2 seven   ......   **6** nine   ......

3 twelve   ......   **7** eighteen   ......

4 Put the letters in the correct order and write the words for the colours.

    DER   ....red........

1 LUEB   ....

2 LLOWEY   ....

3 NEERG   ....

4 GEORAN   ....

5 CLABK   ....

5 Put the words in the correct order.

old / How / you / are?
How old are you?....................................

1 I / understand / don't.

....

2 your / name / What's?

....

3 name's / My / Daniel.

....

4 you / do / How / spell / that?

....

5 your / favourite / What's / colour?

....

6 favourite / My / number / is / seven.

....

6 Write the words in the family tree.

uncle   cousin   ~~grandfather~~   mother

father   sister

.grandfather. and grandmother

.... and .... and aunt

brother   ....   Jack   ....

Hello, I'm Jack.

This is my family.

Write your total score: ...... / 30

1

Countries and nationalities

1 Listen to the countries and nationalities. 🎧

2 Which words are the same in your language?

Come inside!

1

Hi!

- Present simple of *be*
- Introducing yourself
- Talking about nationality

Listen and read

1 Listen to Ricky's first day at school.

Ricky	I'm Ricky Gomez.
Mrs Wilson	Hello. I'm Mrs Wilson. You're in my tutor group. Come in.
Ricky	Thank you.

Mrs Wilson	Good morning, everybody.
Children	Good morning, Mrs Wilson.
Mrs Wilson	This is Ricky Gomez. Welcome to Longfield School, Ricky.
Ricky	Thanks. Hi!
Children	Hi!

Mel   He's American!

Comprehension

2 Write the names of the people in each photo.

1 Hello, I'm ....Sara........   **4** Hi, I'm ....
2 Hi, I'm ....   **5** Hello, I'm ....
3 Hello, I'm ....   **6** Hello, I'm ....

Grammar focus

Present simple of *be*: affirmative

Find the short forms in the dialogue and write them in the chart.

Long form	Short form
I am (Ricky).	....I'm......
You are	....
He is	....
We are	....
You are	..You're..
They are	....

Write the short forms of:
a) She is   ....
b) It is   ....

Nick Let's play football.
Laurie OK.

Mrs Wilson Goodbye, everybody. See you tomorrow.
Nick Goodbye, Mrs Wilson.

Sara Come on, Ricky. We're Manchester United and they're Chelsea!

Grammar practice

3 **Complete the sentences with the short form of *be*.**

1 Ricky **'s**................. American.
2 I .... Sara.
3 She .... Mel.
4 They .... from Malton.
5 You .... Polish.

Now use the long form.

6 Sara and Mel ......**are**......... English.
7 Ricky Gomez .... American.
8 Nick and I .... in Mrs Wilson's tutor group.
9 Mrs Wilson .... the teacher.
10 You and Mel .... 11.

Pronunciation

Words which rhyme

4a **Match the words which rhyme.**

hi see you I
blue play yellow
hello they we

4b **Now listen and check.**

4c **B rhymes with *we*, A with *play* and U with *blue*. Which other words rhyme with letters of the alphabet?**

Talk time

5 **Listen and repeat.**

1 Hello./Hi.
2 Come in.
3 Thank you./Thanks.
4 Good morning.
5 Welcome!
6 Goodbye.
7 See you tomorrow.

1

Are you good at football?

Let's start.

 Listen and read

6 **Listen to the dialogues.**

Mel	Am I in your team?
Sara	Yes, you are.
Nick	Laurie isn't here. Where is he?
Sara	He's over there.
Nick	Come on, Laurie.
Laurie	I'm not ready.
Mel	Are you good at football, Ricky?
Ricky	Good? I'm brilliant! Who's your favourite footballer?
Mel	David Beckham.
Ricky	Who's he? Is he German?
Mel	No, he isn't. He's English.
Sara	Let's start!

Comprehension

7 **True or false?**

	True	False
1 Mel and Sara are in the same team.	✓	
2 Laurie is ready.		
3 Ricky is very good at football.		
4 David Beckham is a footballer.		
5 David Beckham is German.		

Grammar focus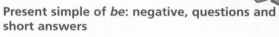

Present simple of *be*: negative, questions and short answers
Complete the table.

Negative	Questions
.I'm. not (ready).	.Am. I (ready)?
You aren't	.... you?
He isn't	Is he?
She	.... she?
It isn't	Is it?
We aren't	Are we?
You	Are you?
They aren't	Are they?

Short answers

Yes, I am.	No, I'm not.
Yes, you	No, you aren't.
Yes, he is.	No, he ....
Yes, she is.	No, she isn't.
Yes, it is.	No, it ....
Yes, we are.	No, we aren't.
Yes, you are.	No, you aren't.
Yes, they are.	No, they ....

I'm not ready.

9 **Listen and complete the school register.**

✓ = here   ✗ = not here

School Register

Mel Brown	✓
Adam Clarke	
Ricky Gomez	
Emma Hardy	
Cherelle Johnson	
Michael Johnson	
Nick Mortimer	

Grammar practice

8a **Complete the sentences.**

1 You .....**are**.n't English.
2 She ....n't here today.
3 We ....n't ready.
4 I .... not in your class.
5 They ....n't at school.
6 .... she good at football?
7 .... you 11?
8 .... we in your team?
9 .... you ready?
10 .... Ricky American?

8b **Complete the questions and answers.**

1 **Are**.... Liverpool and Leeds in Britain?
Yes, **they are**... .
2 .... Leonardo DiCaprio Polish?
No, ...
3 .... Washington DC the capital of the USA?
Yes, ...
4 .... Kylie Minogue American?
No, ...
5 .... you and your friend English?
No, we ....

10 **Ask and answer questions.**

A Is Mel Brown at school today?

B Yes, she is. Is Adam Clarke at school today?

A ....

Write

11 **Now write about students in your class.**

Robert Melandri isn't at school today...........
....
....
....
....
....

Read and write

12 **Write the words in the correct column.**

	Flag	Word
		Polish Poland
		Portuguese Portugal
		France French
		German Germany
		England English
		Japan Japanese
		American The USA
		Australian Australia
		Argentina Argentinian
		Russia Russian

	Country	Nationality
1	Poland	Polish
2		
3		
4		
5		
6		
7		
8		
9		
10		

Listen

13 **Listen and tick (✓) the correct nationality.**

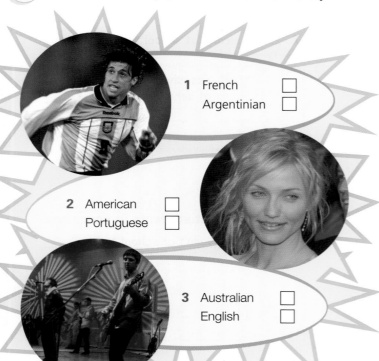

1 French ☐
  Argentinian ☐

2 American ☐
  Portuguese ☐

3 Australian ☐
  English ☐

Write

14 **Complete the dialogues.**

A Who's your favourite footballer?

B Hernán Crespo.

A Is he French?

B No, he isn't. He's Argentinian.

A Who's your favourite film star?

B Cameron Diaz.

A ....?

B ....

A Who's your favourite band?

B Oasis.

A .... they ....?

B ....

Extra!

15 **Work with a partner. Talk about your favourite sports star, film star or band.**

Portfolio

16 **Write about your favourite star. Go to page 130.**

Word Games

1 Colour the sentences that are about you.

I'm ten.

I'm from Portugal.

I'm not English.

I'm eleven.

I'm Russian.

I'm good at football.

I'm twelve.

I'm not American.

I'm a sports star.

I'm from Poland.

2a Circle eight numbers in the snake.

SIXTWOSEVENONEFIVETHREEFOUREIGHT

2b Now write the numbers in the correct order.

....

....

....

....

3 Use the letters to write a list of countries and nationalities. How many can you write in five minutes? You can use the letters more than once.

A   C   D

E   G

I   F

L   H   J

M   T   N

P   R   S

O   U   Y

Clue

There are 10 countries and 10 nationalities.

Culture spot

Schools in Britain

Read

1 Read the information about schools in Britain. Underline the words that you don't know.

Assembly

After-school activities

The school day at Longfield School

Lessons are from Monday to Friday.

School starts	Registration/ Assembly	Morning lessons		Lunch	Registration
8.55	9.00	9.15	Period 1	12.30	1.45
		10.15	Period 2		
		11.15	Break		
		11.30	Period 3		

Afternoon lessons		School finishes	After-school activities
1.50	Period 4	3.50	4.00 - 6.00
2.50	Period 5		

The school year

Term 1	(7 weeks) September to October
Holiday	1 week
Term 2	(7 weeks) November to December
Holiday	2 weeks
Term 3	(6 weeks) January to February
Holiday	1 week
Term 4	(6 weeks) February to April
Holiday	2 weeks
Term 5	(6 weeks) April to May
Holiday	1 week
Term 6	(6 weeks) June to July
Holiday	5 weeks

Types of school, ages of students and year groups

Longfield School is a secondary school. Nick, Ricky, Laurie, Sara and Mel are all 11. They're in Year 7.

Type of school	Ages	Year
Primary	5	1
	6	2
	7	3
	8	4
	9	5
	10	6

	Ages	Year
Secondary	11	7
	12	8
	13	9
	14	10
	15	11
	16	12
	17	13

You can leave school at 16, but most students stay until they are 18.

2 Work with a partner. Can you understand the meaning of the words that you don't know? Check with your teacher.

Comprehension

3 Work with a partner. Answer the questions.

1 Do children in Britain go to school on Saturday morning?
2 At what time does school start/finish in Britain?
3 How many lessons do children have every day?
4 How long is each lesson?
5 How much holiday do children in Britain have?

Write

4 Complete the form.

Schools in my country

The school day at my school

School starts ....

Morning lessons ....

Lunch ....

Afternoon lessons ....

School finishes ....

After-school activities ....

Holidays

	Longfield School	My school
Christmas	about 2 weeks	....
Easter	....	....
Summer	....	....

Types of school

In your country, when do children go from primary to secondary school?

....

....

Are you a film star?

1 **Listen and read.** 🎧

This is Mrs Bennet. She's from The Wizard Film Company.

At school

Good morning, children.

Good morning, Mrs Bennet.

Hello, I'm Nick. I'm from Malton.

At home

Hi, I'm Ricky. I'm not from Malton. I'm American.

Hi. I'm Sara. I'm 11.

Hello, my name's Merlin. I'm a wizard. I'm 110!

Quiet please! This is Nick Mortimer. He's 11.

2a **Answer the questions using the sentences in the box.**

> Yes, he is./No, he isn't.
> Yes, she is./No, she isn't.

1 Is Nick from Malton? ..Yes, he is....
2 Is Mrs Bennet the teacher?
3 Is Ricky from Malton?
4 Is Sara twelve?
5 Is Nick 110?

2b **When the answer is *No*, give the correct information, choosing from the sentences below.**

He's eleven.
She's eleven.
He's from America.
She's from The Wizard Film Company.

2

My school things

1 Listen and look at the pictures. 🎧

2 Listen again and write in the words. 🎧

What do you notice about the plural form of *dictionary*?

dictionary   dictionaries

School subjects

1 a school bag

2 .... 3 .... 4 ....

5 .... 6 .... 7 .... 8 ....

9 .... 10 .... 11 .... 12 ....

a school bag	a ruler	a file
a pencil case	a sharpener	a dictionary
a pencil	a rubber	an exercise book
a pen	a calculator	a packet of sweets

1   2   3

4   5   6

7   8   9

10   11

3 Listen to the words for school subjects. 🎧

4 Listen again and match the words to the pictures. 🎧

Maths ....
History ....
Geography ....
Science ....
Music ....
Art ...1...
PE (Physical Education) ....
DT (Design and Technology) ....
French/German/Portuguese ....
IT (Information Technology) ....
English ....

Have you got everything?

- *have got*
- **Asking and talking about family and possessions**
- **Talking about school subjects and the school timetable**

Listen and read

1 **Listen to Laurie getting ready for school.**

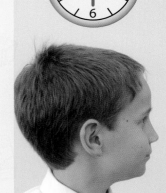

Mum	OK, have you got everything?
Laurie	Yes!
Mum	Have you got your file?
Laurie	Yes, I have.
Mum	Have you got your ruler?
Laurie	Yes, Mum.
Mum	Have you got your dictionary? You've got English today.
Laurie	Yes!
Mum	Have you got your calculator?
Laurie	Yes, Mum. I've got everything. Bye!
Mum	Laurie!
Laurie	Yes.
Mum	You haven't got your pencil case.
Laurie	Oh ... thanks, Mum. Bye. See you later.

Comprehension

2 **Tick the items Laurie is taking to school.**

☐    ☑

☐    ☐

☐    ☐

Grammar focus

The verb *have got*: affirmative and negative

Complete the table.

Affirmative	Negative
I've got (everything)	I haven't got
You've got	You .... got
He's/She's/It's got	He/She/It hasn't got
We've got	We haven't got
You've got	You haven't got
They've got	They haven't got

Grammar practice

(3) **Complete the sentences.**

1 ✓ We've .got......... an Italian sports car.
2 ✗ We .haven't got. a radio.
3 ✓ I'.................. a packet of sweets.
4 ✗ I .... my exercise book.
5 ✓ They'.................. a dictionary.
6 ✗ You .... a pencil.
7 ✓ I'.................. a poster of my
   favourite footballer.
8 ✓ You'.................. my pencil case!

Pronunciation
/h/

(4a) **Listen and repeat.**

1 hello   4 have
2 hi   5 has
3 he   6 History

(4b) **Work with a partner. Repeat the words in exercise 4a. Can you hear the /h/ sound?**

(4c) **How many other words can you think of that begin with the /h/ sound?**

holiday....

Grammar focus

have got: questions and short answers

Complete the table.

Questions	Short answers
Have I got (my file)?	Yes, I ..../No, I haven't.
.... you got?	Yes, you have./No, you haven't.
Has he got?	Yes, he has./No, he hasn't.
Has she got?	Yes, she has./No, she hasn't.
Has it got?	Yes, it has./No, it hasn't.
Have we got?	Yes, we have./No, we haven't.
Have you got?	Yes, you have./No, you haven't.
Have they got?	Yes, they have./No, they haven't.

(5) **Write the questions and answers.**

1 you / pencil case ?
   Have you got a pencil case? Yes, I have..........
2 we / a dictionary ?
   .... No, we ....
3 they / a cat ?
   .... Yes, they ....
4 you / my sweets ?
   .... No, I ....
5 you / a dog ?
   .... Yes, we ....
6 you / my pencil case ?
   .... Yes, I ....

Speak

(6) **Ask and answer questions.**

> **A** Have you got a file in your bag?

> **B** Yes, I have./No, I haven't.

Extra!

(7a) **What have you got in your school bag? Write the names of three items you have got and three items you haven't got.**

I've got a pencil case ... I haven't got a ...

(7b) **Now write about your partner's school bag.**

She's/He's got a ... She/He hasn't got a ...

2

Listen and read

8 **Listen to Ricky and his mother talking about Laurie's family.**

Ricky Mum, Laurie's got a dog.

Mum Mmm.

Ricky She's called Betty. She's really cute. And he's got a cat.

Mum Really?

Ricky Mum! I haven't got a pet.

Mum Has Laurie got brothers and sisters?

Ricky Yes, he's got two brothers.

Mum Oh, that's nice.

Ricky I haven't got a brother or a pet.

Mum You've got a sister, Ricky. Laurie hasn't got a sister.

Ricky Hmm! He's lucky!

Comprehension

9 **Which photo is of Laurie and his family?**

Grammar focus

have got: **third person**

Complete the table.

Affirmative	Negative
He's got (a dog).	He hasn't got
She .... got	She .... got
It's got	It hasn't got
Questions	**Short answers**
Has he got?	Yes, he has./No, he hasn't.
Has she got?	Yes, she has./No, she ....
.... it got?	Yes, it ..../No, it hasn't.

Look at these two sentences from the dialogue. Does the *'s* represent the same word?

Laurie's got a dog.   She's really cute.

Write the sentences out in full.

....

....

Grammar practice

10 **Use the words to write sentences.**

+
she brothers
two got
  's

1 She's got two brothers.

+
got   's
he dog
    a

2 ....

a +
sweets 's
of she
  got
packet

3 ....

got a
pencil she
  case
  hasn't

4 She hasn't got a pencil case.

-
hasn't
calculator a
he got

5 ....

she pet
  hasn't
got a

6 ....

?
he got
exercise
book has
  an

7 Has he got an exercise book?

?
brothers she
  got
has and
  sisters

8 ....

a ?
football has
got your
town
team

9 ....

11a **Complete the chart for Laurie.**

Laurie	✓			
Mel				
Nick			✓	
Ricky				
Sara				

11b **Now listen and complete the chart for Mel, Nick, Ricky and Sara.**

Write and speak

12a **Write the questions and answers. Look at the chart in exercise 11a.**

Mel

1 Has Mel got a cat?   Yes, she has.
  Has she got brothers
  and sisters?   No, she hasn't.

Nick

2 Has Nick got a cat?   ....
  ....   He's got a sister.

Ricky

3 ....   No, he hasn't.
  ....   He's got a sister.

Sara

4 Has Sara got a pet?   ....
  ....   Yes, she's got a
                                   brother and a sister.

12b **Work with a partner.**

A Ask B about Laurie, Mel, Nick, Ricky and Sara.
B Without looking at your book, answer A's questions. Then change roles.

A Has Laurie got a pet?

B Yes, he's got a cat and a dog.

Talk time

13a **Listen and repeat.**

See you later.	Really?	OK.
(She's) really cute!	(She's) lucky!	

13b **Choose the correct response.**

1 **A** This is my cat, Fluffy.

B Oh, she's really cute!

2 **A** Bye!

B Bye! ....

3 **A** She's got a red sports car.

B ....

4 **A** Let's play football after school.

B ....

5 **A** He's got five brothers and five sisters.

B ....

2

Speak and write

14a Work in small groups. Draw a chart like this one. Take turns to ask other students about their pets, brothers and sisters.

14b Write about what you found out.

Anna hasn't got a cat. She's got a dog.
....
....
....
....
....
....
....
....

	Anna	Emil	Thomas	Julia

Read and speak

15a Read the timetable and circle the subjects you study at school.

	Period 1	Period 2		Period 3		Period 4	Period 5
Monday	Maths	IT	B	English	L	History	PE
Tuesday	English	Geography	R	Spanish	U	Science	Music
Wednesday	Art	Maths	E	English	N	DT	French
Thursday	Science	History	A	Geography	C	Maths	Spanish
Friday	French	Maths	K	Spanish	H	English	PE

15b Ask and answer questions.

A Which are your favourite school subjects?

B My favourite subjects are ...

A What have we got tomorrow morning/on Friday afternoon?

B We've got ...

Portfolio

16 Find out about a famous person. Go to page 130.

Word Games

1 Write the letters in the boxes. What are the names of Laurie's pets?

1 Laurie's got a .... called Will. b r o t h e r

2 Have you got a ....? ✏ _ _ _ ☐ _

3 He hasn't got a brother but he's got a .... _ _ _ ☐ _ _

4 I've got a packet of .... _ _ _ _ ☐ _

5 Laurie's got a cat and a dog. He's ....! _ _ _ _ ☐

6 Nick's English, Ricky's .... _ ☐ _ _ _ _ _ _

7 .... you got everything? _ ☐ _ _

8 She hasn't .... a calculator. ☐ _ _

9 Have you got a .... ? 🐰 _ _ ☐

10 No, but ....'ve got a cat. ☐

11 Bye, Mum. See you .... _ _ _ ☐ _

2 Look at the picture below. How many objects can you find? Write a list.

....

....

....

....

....

....

....

....

International e-pals

 Listen

1 Mel is helping Sara join an e-pals club.
Listen and complete the form.

e-pals

YOUR DETAILS

HOME
LOG-IN
LOG-OUT
CHAT
HELP

Name .... **Sara Lawson** ....

Nationality ....

Town/State/County ...**Malton, North Yorkshire**...

Country ....

E-mail address ....@online●.....................

Age ....

Favourite band ..**Blue**....................................

Family ....

Pets ....

Speak

2 Work with a partner. One person is Sara, Ricky, Mel or Nick; the other asks questions.

What's your name?

Where are you from?

What's your e-mail address?

How old are you?

What's your favourite band?

How do you spell that?

Have you got brothers and sisters?

Have you got pets?

Name	Nick Mortimer
Nationality	British
Town, State/County	Malton, North Yorkshire
Country	England
E-mail address	nick@alpha.uk
Age	11
Favourite band	Toploader
Family	sister
Pets	hamster

Name	Mel Brown
Nationality	British
Town, State/County	Malton, North Yorkshire
Country	England
E-mail address	mel@buzz.uk
Age	11
Favourite band	Atomic Kitten
Family	–
Pets	cat

Name	Ricky Gomez
Nationality	American
Town, State/County	Malton, North Yorkshire
Country	England
E-mail address	ricky@beeline.uk
Age	11
Favourite band	Nickelback
Family	sister
Pets	–

Read

3 Read the e-mail and complete the form.

New ▼ | Send | Receive | Forward | Delete

Hi Sara! My name's Ania Swiderska. I'm twelve and I'm Polish. I live in Tyniec, near Krakow. I haven't got any brothers and sisters, but I've got a dog called Kasia. Westlife are my Number 1 band. You can e-mail me on: ania35@polnet.com

Name	....
Nationality	....
Town	....
Country	....
E-mail address	....
Age	....
Favourite band	....
Family	....
Pets	....

Write

4 Complete the form with information about you. Then complete the e-mail.

Name	....
Nationality	....
Town	....
Country	....
E-mail address	....
Age	....
Favourite band	....
Family	....
Pets	....

New ▼ | Send | Receive | Forward | Delete

Hi Sara!

My name's ....

I'm .... and I'm ....

I live in .... I've got/

I haven't got ....

My favourite band is ....

My e-mail .... is ....

Let's check 1

Vocabulary check

1 Circle the correct word.

Britney Spears is from (American /(the USA)).

1 Cristiano Ronaldo is (Portuguese / Portugal).

2 David Beckham and Michael Owen are (England / English).

3 Tokyo is the capital of (Japan / Japanese).

4 'Are you from (Poland / Polish)?'
'No, I'm (Argentina / Argentinian).'

5 Canberra is the capital of (Australia / Australian).

6 Hi! My name's Steffi. I'm (Germany / German).

7 Natasha is (Russian / Russia) and Mitsuko is from (Japan / Japanese).

8 'Is Jennifer Lopez (American / USA)?'

Write your score: .... /10

2 Write in the missing letters. Then match the words to the pictures.

0 p e nc i l
1 c _ lc _ l _ t _ r
2 d _ _ ti _ na _ y
3 f _ l _
4 p _ n
5 _ e _ ci _   c _ se
6 r _ b _ er
7 _ u _ er
8 s _ h _ ol   _ a _
9 s _ a _ pe _ er
10 e _ er _ i _ e   b _ ok

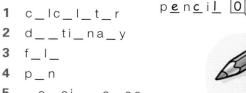

p e nc i l [0]

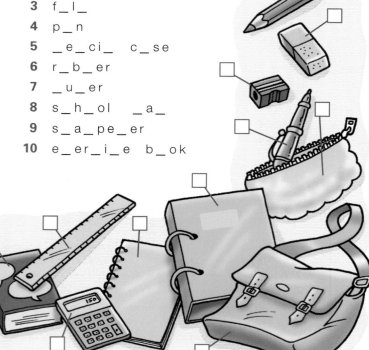

Write your score: .... /20

3 What are these school subjects?

gEshnli	English
1 nieceSc	_____
2 chernF	_____
3 hagyporeG	_____
4 tHrisoy	_____
5 rAt	_____
6 shaMt	_____
7 cuMis	_____
8 Shinsap	_____
9 manGer	_____
10 signeD nda cynoghoTel	_____

Write your score: .... /10

Grammar check

4 Write the short form of the verb be.

My dog is not black. It is brown and white.
My dog isn't black. It's brown and white.

1 I am in class 7A.
....

2 What is the capital of Russia?
....

3 We are in the team.
....

4 I am not Australian.
....

5 Serena is very good at English.
....

6 Who is your favourite band?
....

7 You are in my class.
....

8 My calculator is not in my bag.
....

9 We are not 10.
....

10 We are 11.
....

Write your score: .... /10

5 **Write sentences with *have got*.**

Maria   a brother (✓)   a sister (✗)

Maria's got a brother. She hasn't got a sister.

1 They   a German car (✓)   a French car (✗)

....

....

2 We   Art on Monday (✓)   Science (✗)

....

....

3 Laurie   a pencil (✓)   ruler (✗)

....

....

4 You   Maths today (✓)   English (✗)

....

....

5 I   a white dog (✓)   a white cat (✗)

....

....

Write your score: .... / 10

6 **Look at the chart below. Then complete the questions and short answers.**

	Sandra	Joey and Tony
1 a Ricky Martin CD	✓	✗
2 a poster of Britney Spears	✗	✓
3 a Robbie Williams CD	✓	✗

1 a) *Has* .... Sandra ..*got*............ a Ricky Martin CD?
 Yes, *she has.* ......

 b) *Have* .... Joey and Tony .... a Ricky Martin CD?
 No, ...

2 a) .... Sandra .... a poster of Britney Spears?
 No, ...

 b) .... Joey and Tony .... a poster of Britney Spears?
 Yes, ...

3 a) .... a Robbie Williams CD? Yes, she has.

 b) .... a Robbie Williams CD? No, they haven't.

Write your score: .... / 10

7 **Complete the sentences with the correct words.**

Suzy   ......*Are*....... you good at music?
 A Have   **B** Is   **C** Are ⟵

Alex   Yes, (**1**) ....
 A I'm   **B** I am   **C** it is

 Are (**2**) ....?
 A she   **B** it   **C** you

Suzy   No, but my brother (**3**) .... very good.
 A it's   **B** is   **C** has

 (**4**) .... in a band.
 A She's   **B** He's   **C** He

Alex   Really?

Suzy   Yes. (**5**) .... you got a brother?
 A Are   **B** Has   **C** Have

Alex   Yes, I (**6**) .... He's called Rob.
 A am   **B** have   **C** Has

Suzy   What (**7**) .... got in your bag?
 A have you   **B** you have   **C** you

Alex   My school things and (**8**) .... apple.
 A a   **B** an   **C** two

Suzy   (**9**) .... got a bag of sweets.
 A I'm   **B** I   **C** I've

Alex   (**10**) .... lucky!
 A You're   **B** You've   **C** You

Write your score: .... / 10

Write your total score: .... / 80

You're good at music.

2 It's a Dog's Life!

1 Listen and read. 🎧

2 Find the correct answer for each question.

1 Has Charlie got a brother? ..b..
2 Has she got a sister? ......
3 Has Kevin got a sister? ......
4 Have Kevin and Charlie got a dog? ......
5 Has the dog got the remote control in picture 5? ......
6 Have Mr and Mrs Smith got pets? ......

a No, they haven't.
b Yes, she has.
c Yes, they have.
d No, she hasn't.
e No, it hasn't.
f Yes, he has.

My house

1 Listen to the words for rooms in a house. 🎧

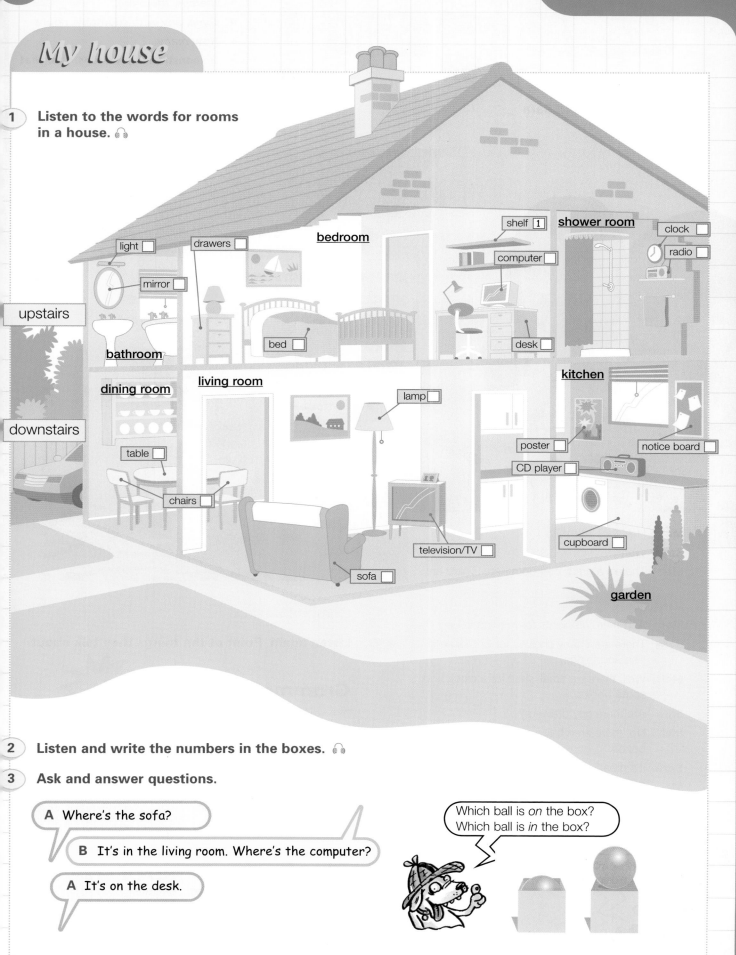

2 Listen and write the numbers in the boxes. 🎧

3 Ask and answer questions.

A Where's the sofa?

B It's in the living room. Where's the computer?

A It's on the desk.

Which ball is *on* the box?
Which ball is *in* the box?

3

This is my room

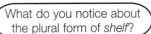

🎧 Listen and read

1 Listen to Mel and Sara.

- there is, there are
- some, any with countable nouns
- How many...?
- Demonstrative pronouns: this, that
- The genitives 's, s'
- Possessive adjectives: my, your...
- Describing rooms and furniture
- Counting from 20 to 1000

Mel	Hey, look at this!
Sara	What?
Mel	There's a great bedroom here. There are two beds.
Sara	Yes.
Mel	And there are lights for reading in bed.
Sara	There aren't any shelves for books and files and things.
Mel	Well, there's a small shelf for a clock and some books.
Sara	Are there any drawers?
Mel	No, there aren't. But there are some boxes.
Sara	It's great!
Mel	Dad!
Dad	The answer's 'No'!

What do you notice about the plural form of *shelf*?

shelf   shelves

Comprehension

2 Listen again. Point at the things they talk about.

Grammar focus

there is/there are

Affirmative	**Negative**
Singular	
There's a bed.	There isn't a bed.
Plural	
There are lights.	There aren't any lights.
Questions	**Short answers**
Is there a desk?	Yes, there is./No, there isn't.
Are there any lamps?	Yes, there are./ No, there aren't.

Read the dialogue again. How many examples of *there is* and *there are* can you find?

42

Grammar practice

3 **Complete the sentences.**

1 There .'s................ a pen on the table.
2 There .are............ two bathrooms upstairs.
3 .... there a dictionary in the classroom?
No, there ....
4 There .... a TV in the living room.
5 .... there thirty students in your class?
Yes, there ....
6 .... a computer in your classroom?
No, there ....

Speak

4 **Tick the things you've got in your bedroom. Then ask your partner about his/her room and complete the chart.**

A Is there a bed in your room?

B Yes, there is.

A Is there a desk?

	My room	*My partner's room*
bed		
desk		
lamp		
notice board		
clock		
radio		
TV		

Grammar focus

some and any

some
You use *some* in affirmative sentences with plural nouns.

There are some books on the shelf.

any
You usually use *any* in negative sentences and in questions with plural nouns.

There aren't any posters in the bedroom.
Are there any posters in the bedroom?

How do you say *some* in your language?
How do you say *any*?

Grammar practice

5 **Complete the sentences.**

1 There are ....some........ pencils in the pencil case.
2 Are there .... shelves in your bedroom?
3 There are .... sweets on the table.
4 Are there .... CDs on the desk?
5 There aren't .... chairs in my bedroom.
6 Are there .... dictionaries in the classroom?
7 There aren't .... cupboards in my room.
8 I've got .... sweets in my bag.

Write and speak

6 **Write questions about the room on page 42. Then ask and answer questions.**

A Are there any posters in the room?

B No, there aren't.

A Are there any shelves?

Speak

7 **Work with a partner. Look at the picture, then close your books and ask and answer questions about it.**

Extra!

8 **Describe your bedroom.**

In my bedroom, there's a/there isn't a ....
There are some .... There aren't any ....
....
....

3

Listen and read

9 **Listen to Nick describing his house.**

Hello, I'm Nick and this is my house. There's a living room. And that's our new TV. It's big! There's a dining room. There's a kitchen. Upstairs there are three bedrooms. This is my mum and dad's bedroom. Their bathroom is here. This is my sister's bedroom. It's quite small. Her favourite colour is pink. Yuck! There's a shower room. There's a toilet. And this is my room. And here's my hamster. His name's Harry. His cage is quite big.

Comprehension

10 **Who says each sentence?**

hamster	mum and dad
Nick	sister

1 'This is my sister's bedroom.' ....Nick............

2 'My favourite colour is pink.'

3 'My name is Harry.'

4 'We've got a bedroom with a bathroom.'

5 'My cage is quite big.'

how many

How many rooms are there in Nick's house?

this/that

That's my house.

This is my house.

Match the sentences to the pictures.

A That's my garden.
B This is my garden.

Grammar focus

The possessive

Nick   his hamster
            Nick's hamster

Sara   her cat
            Sara's cat

Look at these two sentences.

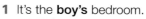

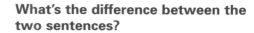

1 It's the **boy's** bedroom.
2 It's the **boys'** bedroom.

What's the difference between the two sentences?

Grammar practice

11 **Who do these things belong to?**

1 Laurie
2 Mel
3 Ricky
4 Nick
5 Sara

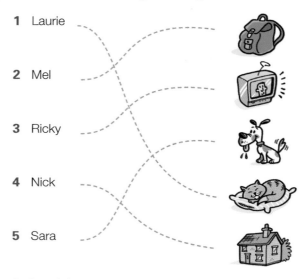

1 Laurie's cat

Talk time

12a **Listen and repeat.**

1	Oh yes.	4	What?
2	Look at this!	5	Yuck!
3	It's great!		

12b **Now complete the dialogue.**

A Hey, look at this!

B ....

A This new computer.

B .... My sister's got a computer.

A Really?

B Yes. .... But, it's green!

A Green! ....

12c **Listen and check.**

3

🎧 Listen

13 **Where is Nick? Listen to the sounds and write the answers.**

He's in the living room.	....
He's in his bedroom.	....
He's in the shower room.	.........1.........
He's in the toilet.	....
He's in the kitchen.	....

Grammar focus

Possessive adjectives

Look at the description of Nick's house on page 44. Which of these words can you find?

my, your, his, her, our, their

Which word can't you find? ....

Write a sentence using the missing word.

Complete the table.

Personal pronouns	Possessive adjectives
I	
you	your
he	his
she	
it	its
we	
you	
they	their

Grammar practice

14a **Sara is talking about her house. Use a possessive adjective to complete the sentences.**

1 Hello, I'm Sara and this is ....**my**......... house.

2 This is my brother's room. .... favourite colours are orange and purple. Yuck!

3 We've got a big living room but .... TV is really small.

4 My mum and dad have got a big bedroom. And this is .... bathroom.

5 Have you got a TV in .... bedroom?

6 My sister's got a TV in .... bedroom. Lucky thing!

14b **Work it out!**

1 How many TVs are there in Sara's house?

2 How many bedrooms are there?

🎧 Pronunciation
/ʌ/

15 **Listen and repeat the /ʌ/ sound.**

1 c<u>u</u>pboard	**4** m<u>u</u>m	**7** h<u>u</u>ndred
2 <u>u</u>ncle	**5** c<u>ou</u>sin	**8** y<u>u</u>ck
3 m<u>o</u>ther	**6** br<u>o</u>ther	**9** l<u>u</u>cky

Speak

16 **Work with a partner. Look at the photo of Nick's family. Who are the people?**

Number 1 is Nick's grandmother. Her name's Pat.

Number 2 is ....

my grandmother - Pat
my grandfather - David
my aunt - Sue
my uncle - Fred
my cousins - Helen and Mathew

Write and speak

17a **Write the names of people in your family.**

17b **Ask and answer questions.**

A How many cousins have you got? What are their names?

B My cousins' names are Claire and Julia.

46

1 Listen to the numbers. 🎧

20	**twenty**
21	**twenty-one**
22	**twenty-two**
23	**twenty-three**
24	**twenty-four**
25	**twenty-five**
26	**twenty-six**
27	**twenty-seven**
28	**twenty-eight**
29	**twenty-nine**
30	**thirty**
40	**forty**
50	**fifty**
60	**sixty**
70	**seventy**
80	**eighty**
90	**ninety**
100	**a hundred/one hundred**
101	**a hundred and one**
200	**two hundred**
1000	**a thousand/one thousand**

2a Listen and circle the numbers. 🎧

38	41	45	53
69	71	78	82
93	97	105	110
225	357	414	999

2b Which numbers are not circled?
Add them up. ....

2c Find the answer in these letters.

3 Choose the correct answer.

1 How many metres are there in ten kilometres?
 a A hundred.
 b A thousand.
 c Ten thousand.

2 How many footballers are there in two teams?
 a Eleven.
 b Thirty.
 c Twenty-two.

3 How many dalmatians are there in the film?
 a A thousand and one.
 b Ninety-nine.
 c A hundred and one.

4 How many states are there in the United States?
 a Fifty-one.
 b Fifty.
 c Forty-nine.

5 How many days are there in a year?
 a Six hundred and thirty-five.
 b Three hundred and fifty-six.
 c Three hundred and sixty-five.

Culture spot
From a tree house ....

Read

1 **Read about Adam's house.**

This is my tree house.

dam **McIntosh**, 15, lives in Edinburgh, Scotland. His house, Sycamore Towers, is not a normal house. It's a tree house. It's quite small – in fact, it's just one room. But there's a kitchen area and there's a shower. He's got a stereo and he's even got a carpet. And it's quite warm. Why? Because it's got solar-powered heating.

'**It's really weird,**' says one of his friends.

'**No, it's not. It's great!**' says another friend.

Vocabulary

3 **What are the pictures?**

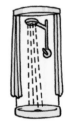

1 <u>a tree house</u>   2 ....

Comprehension

2 **Answer the questions.**

1 What's Adam's surname? ..McIntosh..

2 How old is Adam?

3 Where is he from?

4 What's his house called?

5 Why is his house special?

6 Why is the house warm?

7 Describe his house.

3 ....   4 ....

... to the White House

4 **Look at the picture of the White House and answer the questions.**

1 Where is the White House?
   a) It's in the USA.
   b) It's in France.
   c) It's in Russia.

2 Whose house is it?
   a) It's the Queen's house.
   b) It's the President's house.
   c) It's the Prime Minister's house.

5 **Read the questions about the White House and try to guess the answers.**

1 How many rooms are there? ....

2 How many bathrooms are there? ....

3 How many doors are there? ....

4 How many windows are there? ....

5 How many visitors are there each day? ....

Listen

6a **Listen and write the numbers.**

So, ladies and gentlemen, welcome to the White House, the home of the President of the United States of America.

Before we begin our tour of the White House, let me give you a few facts and figures.

Now, it's quite a big place. In the White House, there are ....132......... rooms. There are .... bathrooms – yes .... And there are .... doors and .... windows.

Every day, there are about .... visitors.

So, that's enough facts and figures. Let's look at the house.

6b **How many answers did you guess correctly?**

Write

7 **Describe a large house that you know.**

Portfolio

8 **Imagine your ideal house. Write the names of the rooms. Go to page 131.**

3

The school visitor

1 **Listen and read.** 🎧

- Sit down please!
- Quiet now, Melanie.
- But sir, Nick's got ...
- He's so cute!
- Be careful!
- Oh, look!
- Look, Ricky, it's on the desk.

3
- This is ridiculous! Sara, Ricky, what's so funny?
- It's in his pocket.
- It's Nick's hamster, sir.

4
- Is there a hamster in your pocket, Nick?
- Yes, sir. It's for Science, sir. It's for my talk on hamsters. They're very interesting animals.

5
- I'm sure they are. But put the hamster in its cage now, please.
- Yes, sir.

2 **Complete the sentences.**

on the desk	in class	on hamsters
in its cage	in his pocket	

1 Nick, Ricky, Sara, Laurie and Mel are
....

2 Sara says: 'Look, Ricky, it's ....'

3 Ricky says: 'It's Nick's hamster, sir.' Sara says:
'It's ....'

4 Nick's got his hamster at school for his Science
talk ....

5 The teacher says: 'Put the hamster
....'

3 **Who is the school visitor?**
Can you remember his name?

4

Months

1 **Listen to the months.** 🎧

 January
 February
 March
 April
 May
 June
 July
 August
 September
 October
 November
 December

 Months always start with a capital letter.

2 **Listen and write the months.** 🎧

1 My birthday's in ..October.... .

2 My birthday's in ....

3 My birthday's in ....

4 My birthday's in ....

Dates

1st	first	17th	seventeenth
2nd	second	18th	eighteenth
3rd	third	19th	nineteenth
4th	fourth	20th	twentieth
5th	fifth	21st	twenty-first
6th	sixth	22nd	twenty-second
7th	seventh	23rd	twenty-third
8th	eighth	24th	twenty-fourth
9th	ninth	25th	twenty-fifth
10th	tenth	26th	twenty-sixth
11th	eleventh	27th	twenty-seventh
12th	twelfth	28th	twenty-eighth
13th	thirteenth	29th	twenty-ninth
14th	fourteenth	30th	thirtieth
15th	fifteenth	31st	thirty-first
16th	sixteenth		

🎧 Pronunciation

/θ/

3 **Listen and repeat the /θ/ sound.**

1 seventh
2 tenth
3 fourth
4 fifteenth
5 eighteenth
6 twenty-fifth

4 **Listen and circle the dates on the calendar.**

5 **When's your birthday? When are the birthdays of the people in your family?**

My birthday's on the second of May. ....
My brother's birthday is on ....
....
....

4

Can I have a party?

- **can** for permission and possibility
- Verbs: *do, go, have, take*
- Asking permission and talking about possibility
- Asking and saying the time

🎧 Listen and read

1 **Listen to Nick talking to his parents.**

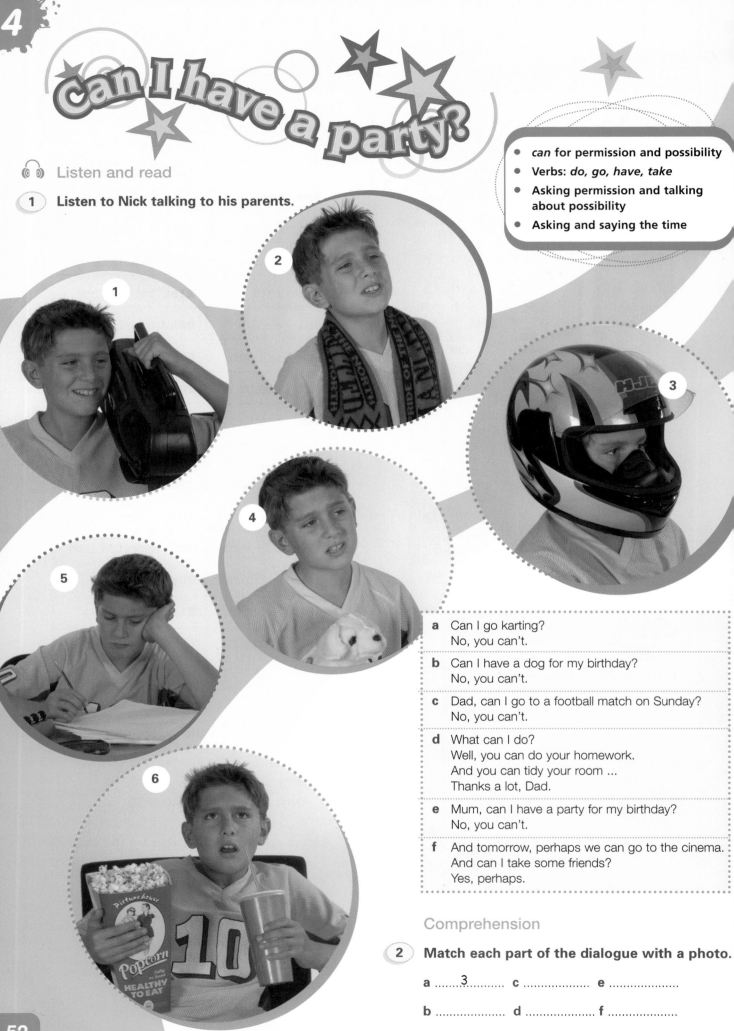

a Can I go karting?
No, you can't.

b Can I have a dog for my birthday?
No, you can't.

c Dad, can I go to a football match on Sunday?
No, you can't.

d What can I do?
Well, you can do your homework.
And you can tidy your room ...
Thanks a lot, Dad.

e Mum, can I have a party for my birthday?
No, you can't.

f And tomorrow, perhaps we can go to the cinema.
And can I take some friends?
Yes, perhaps.

Comprehension

2 **Match each part of the dialogue with a photo.**

a ....3.......... c .... e ....

b .... d .... f ....

52

Grammar focus

can for permission and possibility

Affirmative	Negative	Questions	Short answers
I can (go).	I can't (go).	Can I (go)?	Yes, I can./No, I can't.
You can ...	You can't	Can you ...?	Yes, you can./No, you can't.
He/She/It can ...	He/She/It can't ...	Can he/she/it ...?	Yes, he/she/it can./No, he/she/it can't.
We can ...	We can't	Can we ...?	Yes, we can./No, we can't.
You can ...	You can't ...	Can you ...?	Yes, you can./No, you can't.
They can ...	They can't ...	Can they ...?	Yes, they can./No, they can't.

Grammar practice

3a **Write the words in the correct order to make questions. Then complete the answers.**

1 | go | I | can | the | cinema | to | ? |

<u>Can I go to the cinema?</u>...................

Yes, you .<u>can.</u>...........

2 | we | have | a | can | pet | ? |

....

No, you ....

3 | hamster | my | take | I | to | can | school | ? |

....

No, you ....

3b **Write affirmative sentences.**

4 | karting | go | can | we |

<u>We can go karting.</u>..............................

5 | can | have | they | party | a |

....

6 | can | go | you | a | football match | to |

....

3c **Write negative sentences.**

7 | do | I | can't | homework | my |

<u>I can't do my homework.</u>.....................

8 | can't | she | take | to | school | cat | her |

....

9 | he | go | can't | Saturday | on |

....

4 **Complete the questions with the correct verbs.**

| go | have | take | do |

1 Can I ......<u>take</u>...... some friends to a football match?
2 Can she .... to the cinema?
3 Can he .... a party?
4 Can I .... my homework tomorrow?
5 Can we .... for a pizza?
6 Can I .... my hamster to school?

Extra!

5 **Look at exercise 4. Write three questions to ask your parents when you get home.**

Pronunciation
/æ/ or /ɑː/

6a **Listen and write the words in the correct column.**

1 can't
2 can
3 past
4 thanks
5 class
6 film star
7 packet
8 cat
9 karting

/æ/	/ɑː/
can	can't
....	....
....	....
....	....
....	....

6b **Now listen and check.**

4

(7a) **Listen to Nick's mother inviting Ricky and Mel to a birthday party.**

Nick's mum	Hello, Ricky, it's Nick's mum here.
Ricky	Hi, Mrs Mortimer.
Nick's mum	It's Nick's birthday on Saturday. Can you come to the cinema? It's a surprise!
Ricky	Yes, great. I can come.
Nick's mum	The film's at 5 o'clock. We can go for a pizza afterwards.
Ricky	Great!

Nick's mum	Hello, Mel. How are you?
Mel	I'm fine, thanks.
Nick's mum	Can you come to the cinema with us on Saturday?
Mel	Oh, Saturday ... the 27th of October ...That's Nick's birthday, isn't it? Oh, no, I'm sorry, I can't.
Nick's mum	Oh, never mind.
Mel	Thanks, anyway.

Comprehension

(7b) **Answer the questions.**

1 What date is Nick's birthday?
   The 27th of October.........

2 What time is the film?
3 Can Ricky go to the cinema?
4 Can Ricky go for a pizza?
5 Can Mel go to the cinema?

🎧 Listen

(8) **Now listen to Nick's mother talking to Sara and Laurie on the phone. Answer the question.**

Can Sara and Laurie go?

Speak

9 Work in small groups. Ask and answer questions.

> **B** Is your birthday in June?

> **A** No, it isn't.

> **C** Is it in March?

> **A** No, it isn't.

> **D** Is it in September?

> **A** No, it isn't.
> It's in February!

Listen and speak

10a Listen and write the dates.

1 5 / 11 ....   4 ....

2 ....   5 ....

3 ....   6 ....

10b Work with a partner.

A Write a date.
B Ask the question: What's the date today?
A Answer with: It's the ... of
B Write the answer.
A Check the answer.
Then change roles.

Write

11 Look at the birthday card. Write a similar message for a friend.

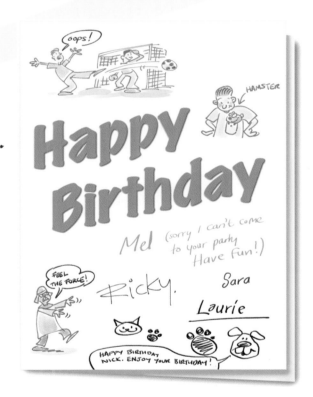

Portfolio

12 Write a birthday message to a famous person. Go to page 131.

4 Time

o'clock
five to   five past
ten to   ten past
quarter to   quarter past
twenty to   twenty past
twenty-five to   twenty-five past
half past

🎧 Listen and read

13 Listen and write the times.

Ricky	What's the time?
Sara	It's .quarter to five..

Sara	It's .... Where are they?
Laurie	Look there they are!
Nick	Oh, hello. Why are you all here?
Laurie	Surprise, surprise! Happy birthday!

Mum	It's .... Time for the film.

Nick	Mum, I'm hungry.
Mum	Well, it's .... I think it's time for a pizza.
All	Yes!

Dad	It's .... Time to go.
Waiter	Excuse me, are you Nick Mortimer? I've got something for you.
Nick	A cake!
Waiter	How old are you, Nick?
Nick	I'm 11. Oh, no, I'm 12.
All	Happy Birthday to you, Happy Birthday to you, Happy Birthday dear Nick, Happy Birthday to you.

Comprehension

14 Answer the questions.

1 Is it a special day? .Yes, it's Nick's birthday.......
2 Where are Nick and his friends at half past five?
3 Where are they at 8 o'clock?
4 What has the waiter got for Nick?
5 How old is Nick today?

Speak

15 Ask and answer questions.

1   2   3

4   5   6

A What time is it?

B It's ....

🎧 Talk time

16a Look again at the dialogues in this unit. Then write the missing words.

1 Perhaps we .can............. (go to the cinema).
2 Thanks .... lot.
3 A How are you?
   B I'm ...., thanks.
4 Oh, ... mind.
5 I'm sorry I .... (come to your party).
6 Surprise, ...!
7 .... Birthday!

16b Now listen and check.

17 Use the dialogues on page 54 to help you write a phone conversation.

A Hi, it's Sara here.
B Hello, Sara. How are you?
A I'm fine, thanks.
A Sara invites B to a party on Friday.
B Accepts the invitation and ask what time the party starts.
A Answers.
B Thanks A.
A Says goodbye.
B Says goodbye.

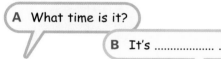

56

Word Games

1   **Match the stars to their birthdays.**

Brad Pitt's birthday is in December.	14/4
Sarah Michelle Gellar's birthday is in April.	24/7
Michael Schumacher's birthday is in the first month of the year.	18/12
Jennifer Lopez's birthday is in the month after June.	3/1

2   **Find all the months of the year in the puzzle.**

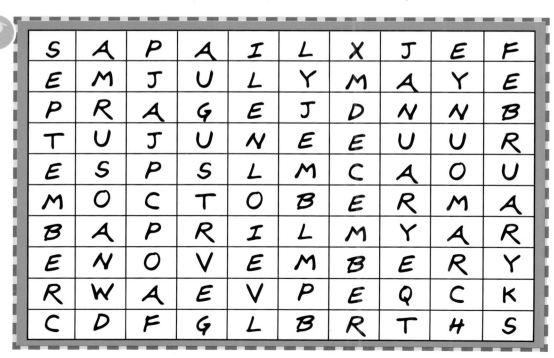

S	A	P	A	I	L	X	J	E	F
E	M	J	U	L	Y	M	A	Y	E
P	R	A	G	E	J	D	N	N	B
T	U	J	U	N	E	E	U	U	R
E	S	P	S	L	M	C	A	O	U
M	O	C	T	O	B	E	R	M	A
B	A	P	R	I	L	M	Y	A	R
E	N	O	V	E	M	B	E	R	Y
R	W	A	E	V	P	E	Q	C	K
C	D	F	G	L	B	R	T	H	S

4

Skills development

Birthdays

🎧 Listen and read

1 Listen and read.

Birthday Bulletin

Happy birthday, Declan!
Hope you like the new CD player.
Now you can play your CDs in
your room!

Love from Mum, Dad and Lauren.

HAPPY BIRTHDAY
11 ON 2nd MAY

Hi, there, Stelios!
You're a real teenager at last!
Have a great birthday.
Can we have some birthday cake?
From all your friends in Class 7HG.

HAPPY BIRTHDAY
13 ON 3rd MAY

Surprise, surprise! The secret's out, Emily.
You're 18 on Friday! That's so old!
Never mind – see you at the party!

From all your mates at Lowood
High School.

HAPPY BIRTHDAY
18 ON 5th MAY

Happy birthday, Charlotte.
Hope you get lots of nice presents.
Clue: there's one in your cupboard,
on the top shelf.

With love from your brother and sister.

HAPPY BIRTHDAY
13 ON 1st MAY

Happy birthday, Tom.
Lots of love from Mum, Dad and Grandma.
There's a surprise in the garden, but you
can't go and live in it!

HAPPY BIRTHDAY
12 ON 4th MAY

58

2 **Match the pictures to the people on page 58.**

1 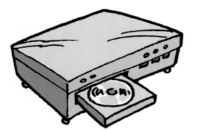 Stelios........

2  ....

3  ....

4 ....

5 ....

 Listen

3 **Whose birthday is it? Listen and write.**

1 It's Charlotte's birthday....
2 ....
3 ....
4 ....
5 ....

Speak

4a **Ask and answer questions.**

A When is Declan's birthday?

B It's the second of May.
   Who's 18 on Friday?

4b **How old are the people? Can you remember?**

A Declan's eleven.

Write

5 **Write a birthday message for a friend.**

Let's check ②

4

Vocabulary check

1 Write the words.

1 ....r

2 ....f

..........phot.o

3 ....d

4 ....e

6 ....d

5 ....k

8 ....p

7 ....k

9 ....s

10 ....r

HAUNTED MANSION

Write your score: .... / 10

60

② **Match the questions to the answers.**

103 + 72 = ..d.. a) seventy-seven
1 87 − 44 = b) eight hundred and seventeen
2 117 − 40 = c) one hundred and twenty-five
3 612 + 205 = d) one hundred and seventy-five
4 150 − 25 = e) two hundred and fifty-nine
5 89 + 170 = f) forty-three

Write your score: …. / 10

③ **Write the birthday dates.**

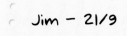

Jim − 21/9

Jim's birthday is on
the twenty-first of
September.

1 Alice − 29/8 ....
2 Sam − 13/3 ....
3 Josie − 1/1 ....
4 Pippa − 22/7 ....
5 Isabel − 11/11 ....

Write your score: …. / 10

④ **What time is it?**

12.00 It's twelve o'clock ....
1 2.20 ....
2 9.45 ....
3 7.30 ....
4 1.05 ....
5 3.50 ....

Write your score: …. / 10

Grammar check

⑤ **Put the words in the correct order.**

a white / garden / There's / cat / our / in
There's a white cat in our garden. ....

1 after / football / play / I / can't / school
....

2 two / Are / SCIENCE / there / in / Cs / ?
....

3 Lollipop / friend's / is / favourite band / My
....

4 great posters / are / in / There / room / her / some
....

5 bag / there / pink sweets / any / Are / in the / ?
....

Write your score: …. / 10

⑥ **Write questions with *Can I* and a verb from the box. Then write short answers.**

| go | have | do | ~~write~~ | be | ~~take~~ | play |

Can I take.............. my hamster to school?
(✗) No, you can't...............................
Can I write.............. with your pen?
(✓) Yes, you can................................

1 .... football with Chris?
(✓) ....
2 .... to the cinema with Alex?
(✓) ....
3 .... a new computer?
(✗) ....
4 .... my homework tomorrow?
(✗) .... Do it today, please.
5 .... in your team?
(✓) ....

Write your score: …. / 20

⑦ **Choose the correct words to complete the sentences.**

...Are.... there any apples in the kitchen?
A Have B Are C Is

1 .... there a clock in your room?
A Are B Is C Has

2 My .... name is Sandra.
A mother's B mothers' C mother

3 There aren't .... posters in her room.
A some B a C any

4 Andy has got a brother. .... birthday is today.
A His B He's C Your

5 In .... house, the computer is in the living room.
A some B a C our

6 My parents have got a TV in .... bedroom.
A their B they're C there

7 There are .... sweets in this drawer.
A some B any C a

8 I've got an American friend. .... name is Maria.
A His B Her C Your

9 Are there .... pictures in your book?
A some B any C a

10 'Can I have a sweet?' 'No, you ....'
A aren't B haven't C can't

Write your score: …. / 10
Write your total score: …. / 80

4

It's a Dog's Life!

1 Listen and read. Then complete the sentences. 🎧

surprise
half past three.
No, you can't.
Yes, you can.
Can we have ...
do your homework.

1 What time is it?

2 Mum, what can we do? — You can .... — It's ....

3 Dad, can we have some crisps? — No, you can't.

4 .... some sweets? — No, you can't!

5 Can we have some cola? — .... Can I have a biscuit?

6 Mum, can we take the dog for a walk? — .... Good idea!

7 Come on, Kevin. — OK.

8 Great idea, Charlie! — Not bad for a girl!

9 Kevin! — Surprise ....

5

Sports

1a Listen and follow. 🎧

1b Listen again and match the words to the pictures. 🎧

1 gymnastics	7 rugby
2 baseball	8 skiing
3 athletics	9 swimming
4 cycling	10 table tennis
5 basketball	11 tennis
6 football	12 volleyball

Free-time activities

2a Listen and follow. 🎧

2b Tick (✓) the activities that you do.

1

☐ I watch TV.

2

☐ I read.

3

☐ I listen to music.

4

☐ I go to the cinema.

5

☐ I go out with my friends.

6

☐ I play the guitar.

7

☐ I play video games.

8
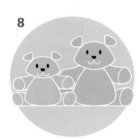
☐ I collect teddy bears.

9

☐ I collect football stickers.

What do you do in your free time?

- Present simple: *like, play, live, read, ...*
- Question words: *Who? What? Where? Why? Which?*
- Talking about free-time activities
- Talking about holidays

Listen and read

1 Listen to Sara talking about her free time.

School magazine — Longfield School

Star profile

Our star student this month is Sara Lawson!

Free time

I read. I like *Harry Potter* books. I watch TV. I go out with my friends. I collect teddy bears. I play football on Mondays and Thursdays.

At the weekend

I go swimming with my friends. We go to Malton pool on Saturdays. I go to see my grandparents on Sundays. They live near Malton.

Hi! I'm Sara Lawson. I'm in Mrs Wilson's class.

1

2

4

3

Comprehension

2 Write a sentence for each photo.

1 I go out with my friends.
2 ....
3 ....
4 ....

Grammar focus

Present simple: affirmative

I play (football).	We play
You play	You play
He/She/It play**s**	They play

When does the verb change in the Present simple? Is it the same in your language?

Grammar practice

3 Complete the sentences with the correct verb.

play   live   read   collect   go   watch

1 You **live**.......... near Malton.
2 I .... tennis.
3 We .... to Longfield School.
4 They .... TV at the weekend.
5 I .... *Harry Potter* books.
6 I .... football posters.

Speak and read

4a Work with a partner. What are the sports?

4b Match the sentences to the pictures.

I play table tennis.	12	I play volleyball.	
I do gymnastics.		I play tennis.	
I play baseball.		I go cycling.	
I go swimming.		I play basketball.	
I play rugby.		I play football.	
I go skiing.		I do athletics.	

Grammar focus

Present simple: third person

He play**s**	He read**s**	He watch**es**
She play**s**	She like**s**	She go**es**
It play**s**	It live**s**	It do**es**

For the third person singular, you add .... or ....

Grammar practice

5 Complete the verbs with *s* or *es*.

1 My dog like.**s**..... TV.
2 She play....... volleyball.
3 He collect....... football stickers.
4 She live....... in Milan.
5 He do....... gymnastics.
6 She do....... athletics.
7 She go....... to her grandparents' at the weekend.
8 He watch.......TV after school.

Listen and speak

6a Listen and complete the chart.

Sara		✓			
Nick					
Mel					
Laurie					
Ricky					

6b Now say what the people do.

Sara goes swimming and she plays football.

5

7 **Listen to the interview with Ricky.**

Mel	Ricky, can we interview you for the school magazine?
Ricky	Sure, no problem.
Sara	What do you do in your free time?
Ricky	I watch TV. I go to the cinema. I play video games.
Sara	OK. Let's talk about sports now. Do you play football?
Ricky	You mean soccer? You bet!
Mel	Do you like American football?
Ricky	No, I don't.
Mel	Do you play baseball and basketball?
Ricky	I play baseball but I don't play basketball.
Sara	I think that's all. Thanks for your help.
Ricky	You're welcome!

Comprehension

8 **Tick (✓) the activities that Ricky does.**

Free-time activities

☐ ☐

☐

☐ ☐

Sports

☐ ☐

☐ ☐

☐ ☐

Write

9 **Complete the sentences.**

★ **Star profile** ★

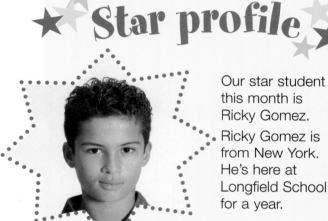

Our star student this month is Ricky Gomez.

Ricky Gomez is from New York. He's here at Longfield School for a year.

Free-time activities

In his free time he ....

....

....

....

Sports

He plays ....

....

He doesn't play ....

....

Grammar focus

Present simple: negative, questions and short answers

Negative	Questions	Short answers	
I don't like (rugby).	Do I like (rugby)?	Yes, I do.	No, I don't.
You don't like …	Do you like …?	Yes, you do.	No, you don't.
He/She/It doesn't like …	Does he/she/it like …?	Yes, he/she/it does.	No, he/she/it doesn't.
We don't like …	Do we like …?	Yes, we do.	No, we don't.
You don't like …	Do you like …?	Yes, you do.	No, you don't.
They don't like …	Do they like …?	Yes, they do.	No, they don't.

I don't play basketball.
Do you like American football?
No, I don't.
What do you do in your free time?

Talk time

10a Complete the dialogues.

1
A Your bike's OK now.
B Thanks for your ...**help** .

2
A Can you help me with my homework now?
B Sure, no ....

3
A Thanks very much.
B You're .... !

4
A Do you like chocolate ice cream?
B You .... !

10b Now listen and check.

10c Practise the dialogues with a partner.

Grammar practice

11a Put the words in the correct order.

1 play / doesn't / he / basketball.
  He doesn't play basketball.
2 she / doesn't / football / like.
3 in / Rome / live / they / don't.
4 you / like / do / skiing?
5 he / does / collect / postcards?
6 don't / we / go / in / December / swimming.
7 does / he / what / do / school / after?
8 do / like / you / why / American / football?

11b Find the mistakes and correct the sentences.

1 Do you likes baseball?   ✗
  Do you like baseball?
2 He don't play basketball.   ✗
  ....
3 She doesn't watches TV.   ✗
  ....
4 They not go to football matches.   ✗
  ....
5 **A** Does he plays volleyball?   ✗
  B Yes, he plays.
  ....
  ....
6 They no like video games.   ✗
  ....

5

Sports profile

Maria Sharapova

 Read and listen

12a Match the questions to the answers.

1 b
Who is Maria Sharapova

2 ☐
Where does she live?

3 ☐
Which sport does she play?

4 ☐
Where does she play?

5 ☐
Why does she like Wimbledon?

6 ☐
What does she do in her free time?

a She plays tennis.

b Maria Sharapova is a sports star.

c She's from Nyagan, in Russia, but she doesn't live there now. She lives in Florida, in the USA.

d She reads. She watches TV. She listens to music, she sings and she does jazz dance.

e She plays in tournaments all over the world. She goes to London in June every year and plays in the Wimbledon championships. She likes Wimbledon.

f Because she plays well on grass.

12b Now listen and check.

Extra!

13 Work with a partner. Talk about what your partner does in his/her free time.

Luke watches TV. He .....

 Pronunciation
/s/ /z/ /ɪz/

14 Listen and repeat.

/s/	/z/	/ɪz/
likes	dogs	watches
sports	goes	kisses
collects	is	
thanks	plays	
	does	

Portfolio

15 Write an article for a magazine. Go to page 132.

Sing a song

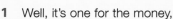

1 **Listen to the song. Find**
  • three numbers • a colour • an animal 🎧

Blue Suede Shoes
by Elvis Presley

1 Well, it's one for the money,

2 Two for the show,

3 Three to get ready,

4 Now go, cat, go.

5 But don't you step on my blue suede shoes.

6 You can do anything

7 But lay off of my blue suede shoes.

8 Well, you can knock me down,

9 Step in my face,

10 Slander my name

11 All over the place.

12 Do anything that you want to do,

13 But uh-uh, honey, lay off of my shoes,

14 But don't you step on my blue suede shoes.

15 You can do anything

16 But lay off of my blue suede shoes.

17 Well, it's one for the money,

18 Two for the show,

19 Three to get ready,

20 Now go, cat, go.

21 But don't you step on my blue suede shoes.

22 You can do anything

23 But lay off of my blue suede shoes.

24 Well, it's blue, blue, blue, suede shoes

25 Blue, blue, blue suede shoes, yeah!

26 Blue, blue, blue suede shoes, baby,

27 Blue, blue, blue suede shoes

28 Well, you can do anything, but lay off of my
    blue suede shoes.

2 Your teacher will give you a line or lines from the song to practise.

3 Practise the song in class without the music. Now sing the song with the music.

5

Culture spot
School holidays

Listen and read

1 **Listen and read. Underline the activities you can do at the activity centre.**

British school children have three main holidays a year: at Christmas, at Easter and in the summer. The summer holiday is about six weeks long.

For their holidays, some children go with their parents to the seaside in Britain. Some go to France, Spain, Italy or other countries. And some go on holiday without their parents – to activity centres.

At an activity centre, you can go swimming, surfing, canoeing, horse riding, and cycling. You can play football, basketball and other sports. You can do archery. You can go karting. You can even try quad biking. You can go to English language classes, too. In the evenings, there are treasure hunts and you sing songs round a camp fire. There are also discos, quizzes and videos.

You stay in tents or in big houses, like the one in the picture. It's called the Mansion House. You can choose to go with children aged eight to ten, or with children aged eleven to thirteen.

There are activity centres in France, too. So you can do all the usual activities and sports, and you can learn French, and you can go on a banana boat!

1 ....

2 ....

Vocabulary

2a **Make two lists with the underlined words.**

Sports and activities

Words I know   Words I don't know

2b **Work with a partner and guess the meaning of the words that you don't know. Then check with your teacher.**

Write

3 **Write sentences for each photo 1–6.**

3 ....

70

4 It's called the Mansion House. ....

5 ....

6 ....

Comprehension

4 **Read the text again. Then answer the questions.**

1 How many outdoor sports and activities can you find?

2 How many indoor sports and activities can you find?

🎧 Listen

5a **Listen to the interview with Patrick. Tick (✔) the things that he does.**

☐ ☐ ☐ ☐ ☐

☐ ☐ ☐ ☐ ☐

5b **Listen again. Why is the house called a 'calendar house'?**

Speak

6 **Ask and answer questions.**

What do you do in the holidays?

Well done, Nick!

1 Listen and read. 🎧

2 Choose the correct answer to each question.

1 Does Nick like football?
2 Does he play for a team?
3 Does he do athletics and gymnastics?
4 Is Nick a good player? What do you think?

Yes, he does.   No, he doesn't.

No, he isn't.   Yes, he is.

3 Underline the correct sentences.

1 Nick likes football./Nick doesn't like football.
2 He plays for a team./He doesn't play for a team.
3 He does athletics and gymnastics too./He doesn't do athletics and gymnastics.
4 He scores a goal./He doesn't score a goal.

6

Daily activities

1 Listen and repeat. 🎧

 **a** I get up at 7 o'clock.

 **b** I have a shower.

 **c** I have breakfast.

 **d** I brush my teeth.

 **e** I go to school.

 **f** I have lunch.

 **g** I get home.

 **h** I do my homework.

 **i** I watch TV.

 **j** I visit my friends.

 **k** I have dinner.

 **l** I go to bed.

 **m** I listen to music.

 **n** I play sport.

 **o** I tidy my room.

 **p** I take the dog for a walk.

 **q** I stay in bed.

 **r** I go to the shops.

 **s** I go out with friends.

 **t** I help at home.

2 Tick (✔) the things you do every day.

3 Put a star (★) next to the things you do *only* at the weekend.

I'm never late for school!

- **Present simple for daily activities**
- **Adverbs of frequency:** *always, usually, often, sometimes, never*
- **Questions with** *ever*
- **Talking about daily activities**
- **Talking about frequency**

Read

1 Read Nick's homework and tick (✔) the activities he mentions.

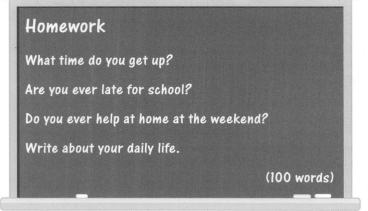

Homework

What time do you get up?

Are you ever late for school?

Do you ever help at home at the weekend?

Write about your daily life.

(100 words)

A Day in My Life

I get up at 6.30. I usually have a shower. I have breakfast. I always brush my teeth after breakfast. I usually walk to school. I'm never late. I'm usually the first to arrive. School's great! We have lunch at 1 o'clock. It's always delicious.

When I get home, I sometimes take the dog for a walk. On school days I never go out with friends. I stay in and do my homework. At the weekend I often help at home.

Nick Mortimer

Grammar focus

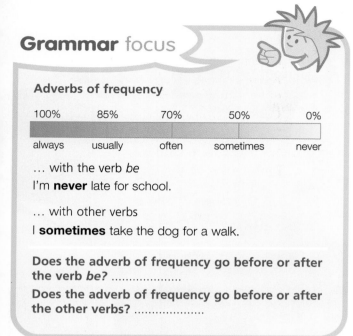

Adverbs of frequency

100%	85%	70%	50%	0%
always	usually	often	sometimes	never

… with the verb *be*
I'm **never** late for school.

… with other verbs
I **sometimes** take the dog for a walk.

Does the adverb of frequency go before or after the verb *be*? ....

Does the adverb of frequency go before or after the other verbs? ....

Grammar practice

2 **Look at Nick's homework and find:**

a sentences with the verb *be* and adverbs of frequency
b sentences with other verbs and adverbs of frequency

 Listen

3 **Listen to Nick's sister and mum talking about his homework. Tick True (T) or False (F).**

		T	F
1	Nick gets up at 6.30.		✓
2	He usually has a shower.		
3	He has breakfast.		
4	He usually walks to school.		
5	Nick's never late for school.		
6	He has lunch at 1 o'clock.		
7	School lunches are always delicious.		
8	He sometimes takes the dog for a walk.		
9	On school days, he never goes out with friends. He stays in and does his homework.		
10	At the weekend, Nick often helps at home.		

4 **Rewrite the sentences putting the adverbs in the correct position.**

1	I get up at about 7.00.	usually
	I usually get up at about 7.00.	
2	I have a shower before breakfast.	usually
3	I go to school by bus.	sometimes
4	I'm late for school.	never
5	I have lunch at school.	always
6	I get home at 3.30.	usually
7	I go out with friends after school.	often
8	I tidy my room at the weekend.	often
9	I'm bored at the weekend.	sometimes
10	I stay in bed on Saturday morning.	never

Write and speak

5a **Now write the sentences again so they are true for you.**

I always get up at about 6.45....

5b **Tell your partner about your routine. Your partner has to complete the chart.**

		always	usually	often	sometimes	never
1						
2						
3						
4						
5						
6						
7						
8						
9						
10						

 Listen and read

6 **Listen to the teacher talking to her class.**

Mrs Wilson	I've got a test for you. It's called, 'Are you a perfect pupil?'
Sara	That's easy! Yes, we're perfect!
Mrs Wilson	Well, let's see. Question 1: Are you ever late for school? Sara?
Sara	No, I'm never late for school.
Mrs Wilson	Question 2: Do you ever forget your homework? Ricky?
Ricky	Homework? Well, I sometimes forget my homework.
Mrs Wilson	Question 3: Laurie, are you ever nervous before a test?
Laurie	Test? What test?
Mrs Wilson	It's OK, Laurie. I think the answer's 'Yes.'
	Question 4: Do you ever draw pictures in class? Mel?
Mel	Yes, I often draw pictures in class. Look!
Mrs Wilson	Question 5: Do you always pay attention in class? Nick? ... Nick! ... Nick!
Nick	I usually pay attention in class. Miss?
Mrs Wilson	What's the matter, Nick?
Nick	Are you ever impatient in class?
Ricky	You're in trouble, Nick!

Comprehension

7 **Match the pictures to the names.**

a

b

c

d

e

f

Sara	.........b.........	Mel	....
Ricky	....	Nick	....
Laurie	....	Mrs Wilson	....

Grammar focus

Questions with *ever*

be

Are you **ever** late for school? No, I'm not./
No, never.

Other verbs

Do you **ever** forget your homework? Yes, I do./
Yes, sometimes.

Translate the sentences into your language.

Grammar practice

8 Put the words in the correct order.

1 you / go to school by car / ever?
   <u>Do you ever go to school by car?</u>

2 he / be late for school / ever?
   <u>Is he ever late for school?</u>

3 you / go swimming on Saturdays / ever?
   ....

4 they / be in Italy in August / ever?
   ....

5 she / listen to the radio before school / ever?
   ....

6 you / be nervous / ever?
   ....

7 we / have homework in the holidays / ever?
   ....

8 he / forget his homework / ever?
   ....

Pronunciation

/ɪ/ /iː/

9a Listen and repeat.

/ɪ/			/iː/			
live	listen	in	she	read	free	please

9b Put these words under the correct sound in exercise 9a. Then listen and check.

he   cinema   sweets
swim   TV   film

Talk time

10a Listen and repeat.

1 Test? What test?   4 What's the matter?
2 You're in trouble,   5 That's easy.
3 Well, let's see.

10b Complete the dialogues.

1 **A** We're really good at Maths.
   B <u>Well, let's see</u>............... .

2 **B** What's the capital of France?
   A .... It's Paris, of course.

3 **A** Oh no!
   B ....?
   A I can't find my school bag.

4 **B** Nick Mortimer, the headteacher wants to see you.
   A .... Nick!

5 **A** Right, listen. This is your English listening test.
   B ....? ....?

10c Now listen and check.

Speak

11 Use the words in the chart to ask and answer questions.

> **A** Do you ever forget your homework?

> **B** Yes, sometimes./No, never./Yes, I often forget my homework.

Do you ever ...	forget	canoeing?
	draw	films in English?
	stay	in bed at the weekend?
	play	in class?
	go	pictures in class?
	sing	rugby?
	watch	your homework?
Are you ever ...	impatient	for/at school?
	nervous	at night?
	late	at home?
	bored	before a test?

6

Read

12 Read about Emma Kai.

Hello! I'm Emma. I live in Tokyo, in Japan. I get up at 7 o'clock. I have breakfast. I cycle to school. It takes a quarter of an hour. School in Japan usually starts at 8.30. We have four lessons before lunch and two after lunch. There's a 15-minute break between the third and fourth lessons. We have 40 minutes for lunch. I always take a packed lunch. School finishes at 3 o'clock. Then we have tutor group time, when our teacher talks to us for 10 to 15 minutes. After that, we clean the classrooms and the corridors. At 4 o'clock there are after-school activities. I sometimes play volleyball or basketball, and I always go to orchestra practice on Wednesday.

Comprehension

13 Complete the chart.

Name:	Emma Kai
Hometown:	
School starts at:	
Number of lessons in the day:	
Lunch:	
School finishes at:	
At 3.00:	
At 3.15:	
At 4.00:	
After-school activities:	

Extra!

14 Look again at Nick's homework on page 74 and write about your day.

I usually get up at...

Portfolio

15 Find information about your favourite star's typical day. Go to page 133.

78

Word Games

1 **Work with a partner. Take turns to ask each other the questions in the quiz. Then look at the analysis.**

Are you a perfect pupil?

1 **Are you ever late for school?**
a I'm never late for school.
b I'm sometimes late for school.
c I'm usually late for school.

4 **Do you ever draw pictures in class?**
a Yes, often.
b Yes, sometimes.
c No, never.

2 **Do you ever forget your homework?**
a Yes, I often forget my homework.
b I sometimes forget my homework.
c No, I never forget my homework.

5 **Do you ever stay up late?**
a No, I never stay up late.
b Yes, I usually stay up late.
c I sometimes stay up late.

3 **Do you always pay attention in class?**
a No, I never pay attention in class.
b Yes, always.
c I usually pay attention in class.

6 **Are you ever in trouble at school?**
a No, I'm never in trouble at school.
b Sometimes, but not often.
c I'm always in trouble at school.

Analysis

Mostly

You're perfect! But are you too good to be true?

Mostly

You're not perfect but you're a good student. Well done!

Mostly

You're often in trouble. Is that right?

6

Skills development

Survey – All about you

Read

1 Mel and Laurie are writing the results of a school survey. Read the survey.

Longfield School Survey   Year 7 (11- and 12-year-olds)

Sports

a How often do you play/do sport?

> 1 Often ...58%..
> 2 Sometimes ....
> 3 Not very often ...2%....

b Which sport do you play/do?

> 4 Football
> 5 Swimming
> 6 ....

Family

c Are you ever in trouble at home? Why?

> 7 Because I never tidy my room.
> 8 Because I ....
> 9 Because I often get up late.
> 10 Because I watch too much TV.
> 11 Because I sometimes raid the fridge.

After-school activities

d What do you usually do after school?

> 12 I play football.
> 13 I play with my friends.
> 14 I go to an after-school club.
> 15 I go swimming.
> 16 ....

Bedtime

e What time do you go to bed on school nights?

> 17 I usually go before 10 p.m.   ....%
> 18 I usually go after 10 p.m.   ....%

f What time do you go to bed during the holidays?

> 19 I usually go before 11 p.m. ....%
> 20 I usually go after 11 p.m. ....%

🎧 Read and listen

2a Can you guess what the missing information on page 80 is?

2b Now listen and check.

	My guess	Correct answer
Sports	2	....
	6	....
Family	8	....
After-school activities	16	....
Bedtime	17	....
	18	....
	19	....
	20	....

Speak and write

3 Work with a partner. Read the survey questions. Then write the answers.

Sports

a How often do you play or do sport?

b Which sport do you play or do?

Family

c Are you ever in trouble at home? Why?

After-school activities

d What do you usually do after school?

Bedtime

e What time do you go to bed on school nights?

f What time do you go to bed during the holidays?

Write

4 Write questions for a class survey. Then show your results like this:

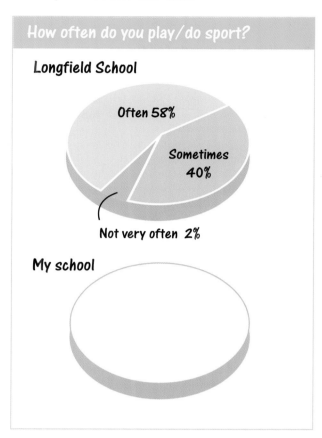

Let's check ③

Vocabulary check

1 **Write the words for the sports.**

bleat nestin
table tennis.

1 kingis

....

2 sinnet

....

3 glycinc

....

4 wingmims

....

5 blotloaf

....

6 gubry

....

7 blakbleats

....

8 labelsab

....

9 cheattils

....

10 mangicysts

....

Write your score: .... / 10

2a **Match the words.**

video	lunch
1 football	bears
2 ice	game
3 packed	sticker
4 teddy	tennis
5 table	cream

2b **Now use the words in these sentences.**

I've got a new .video game. called *Zoom Raider*.

1 It's hot. I want an ....

2 We can play .... in our dining room. We've got a very big table.

3 He always takes a .... to school.

4 Have you got a David Beckham .... ?

5 She's got three cute .... on her bed.

Write your score: .... / 10

Grammar check

3 **Complete the sentences with the verb in the correct form.**

brush	do	~~get~~	go	have	listen
play	stay	take	tidy	watch	

I ..get....... home at four o'clock. My sister **gets.** home at half past four.

1 I .... breakfast in the kitchen. My sister .... breakfast in bed.

2 You .... your teeth after breakfast. My brother .... his teeth after school!

3 You .... football after school. My brother .... video games.

4 I .... gymnastics on TV. Dad .... football.

5 You .... the dog for a walk in the morning. Sam .... the dog for a walk after school.

6 I .... my homework in the living room. My sister .... her homework in the bath.

7 I .... to bed at nine o'clock. My brother .... to bed at ten.

8 I .... to American pop music on the radio. My friend .... to Rock music.

9 I .... up late on Saturday night. My dog never .... up late.

10 You .... your room every day. My mother .... my room.

Write your score: .... / 2

4 Put the words in the correct order.

don't / my / live / school / near / I
I don't live near my school.

1 weekend / Are / bored / the / you / at / ever ?
....

2 ever / your / Does / homework / your / do / mother ?
....

3 matches / am / usually / I / before / nervous
....

4 for / never / My / her breakfast / is / cat / late
....

5 often / bed / music / in / listen / to / I
....

Write your score: …. / 5

5 Choose the correct words to complete the text.

Ben Lyons is 11 and he's Plymouth's new swimming star. Ben ....**gets**..... up at six o'clock every day and (1) …........…. to his swimming club. 'I (2) …........…. for two hours, then I (3)…........…. home for breakfast,' he says. '(4)…........…. in trouble because I'm late for school.' Ben's school (5)…........ at 9.00 and (6)…........…. at 3.30. After school Ben (7)…........…. his homework for an hour. He says, 'I (8)…........…. like homework but I (9)…........…. it.' Then he (10)…........…. his dog, Misty, for a walk on the beach. 'Misty is a cute dog,' Ben says. 'She (11)…........… like swimming but she (12)…........… music. Robbie Williams is her favourite pop star. She sits on my bed and (13)…........…. CDs. Misty and I (14)…........…. up late. (15) …........… in bed at 9.00.'

6 Choose the correct words to complete the sentences.

My grandmother ..**collects**.. teddy bears.
A collect   B collects   C don't collect

1 Our dog …........…. like swimming.
A don't   B isn't   C doesn't

2 Where …........…. you live?
A do   B are   C have

3 …........…. like football?
A Are you   B Do you   C He

4 My parents …........…. play video games.
A don't   B aren't   C not

5 When …........…. Sabrina go to bed?
A has   B does   C is

6 …........…. Nick play baseball?
A Do   B Does   C Is

7 Lucy …........…. her homework.
A never forget   B never forgets   C forgets never

8 Dave …........…. late for school.
A is often   B often is   C often does

9 'Are you ever late for school?' '…........….'
A Yes, I do.   B No, it isn't.   C No, I'm not.

10 'Does Joe like sweets?' '…........….'
A Yes, he likes.   B Yes, it is.   C Yes, he does.

Write your score: …. / 10

	A	B	C
	A get	B gets	C stands
1	A goes	B go	C plays
2	A swim usually	B usually swims	C usually swim
3	A take	B have	C go
4	A I sometimes	B I'm sometimes	C I sometimes am
5	A starts	B starting	C start
6	A finish	B finishs	C finishes
7	A stays	B do	C does
8	A doesn't	B not	C don't
9	A always do	B do always	C always does
10	A take	B does take	C takes
11	A not	B doesn't	C don't
12	A like	B likes	C is like
13	A listens	B listen to	C listens to
14	A stay never	B never stay	C don't never stay
15	A We always	B Always we're	C We're always

Write your score: …. / 15

Write your total score: …. / 70

6

It's a Dog's Life!

1 Read and circle True or False.

1 My cat usually sleeps on my bed. ~~True~~ **(True)** False

2 We're never in trouble. **True** **False**

3 I often tidy my room. **True** **False**

4 My mum sometimes sings in the car. **True** **False**

5 We sometimes stay up late **True** **False**

6 I'm never nervous before a test. **True** **False**

7 They sometimes forget to take me for a walk. **True** **False**

2 Now listen and check. 🎧

84

7

Animals

1 Listen and match the words to the pictures. 🎧

a   armadillo ....
b   chameleon ....
c   cheetah ....
d   chicken ....
e   duck ....
f   elephant ....1....
g   kangaroo ....
h   parrot ....
i   penguin ....
j   polar bear ....
k   ring-tailed lemur ....
l   monkey ....
m   spider ....

be + adjective

2 Listen and read. 🎧

1	I'm hungry.	6	I'm thirsty.
2	I'm tired.	7	I'm right.
3	I'm cold.	8	I'm wrong.
4	I'm hot.	9	I'm angry.
5	I'm frightened.	10	I'm bored.

3a Now match the sentences to the sounds. 🎧

1 ....   3 ....
2 ....   4 ....

3b Which sentences are left? Can you mime them?

7 Can you tap dance?

- *can* for ability
- *be* + adjective
- Talking about ability
- Talking about feelings and states

Listen and read

1 Listen to Nick answering the questions on his audition form below. Tick (✔) his answers to the first four questions.

Nick	Can you help me fill in this audition form?
Sara	OK.
Nick	Thanks! It's from the film company.
Ricky	Oh, that's good.
Sara	Let's see, first question: Can you sing?
Nick	Yes, of course I can.
Ricky	OK, OK, you can sing. Can you dance?
Nick	Yes, I can. Look!
Sara	Hmm. Quite good. Can you tap dance?
Nick	Tap dance?
Sara	Yes, you know, like in the old films.
Nick	Well, not really, no.
Ricky	Never mind. You can dance, but you can't tap dance. That's fine.
Sara	Can you ride a horse, Nick?
Nick	Yes, watch this.
Sara	A real horse, Nick!
Nick	Yes, I can.

WIZARD FILM COMPANY
Audition form

	Nick's answers		My partner's answers	
	Yes	No	Yes	No
Can you sing?	✔			
Can you dance?				
Can you tap dance?				
Can you ride a horse?				
Can you skate?				
Can you swim?				
Can you drive?				
Can you speak French?				

Listen

2 Listen and tick (✔) the answers to the rest of the questions.

Grammar focus

can for ability

Affirmative	Negative
I can (swim).	I can't (swim).
You can	You can't
He/She/It can	He/She/It can't
We can	We can't
You can	You can't
They can	They can't

Questions	Short answers
Can I (go)?	Yes, I can./No, I can't.
Can you ...?	Yes, you can./No, you can't.
Can he/she/it ...?	Yes, he/she/it can. No, he/she/it can't.
Can we ...?	Yes, we can./No, we can't.
Can you ...?	Yes, you can./No, you can't.
Can they ...?	Yes, they can./No, they can't.

How do you say these sentences in your language?

I can swim. I can't sing. Can you ride a horse?

> You use *can* to express ability.

I **can** swim.
Can you tap dance?

> You also use *can* to express possibility. See Unit 4.

She **can't** come to the party on Saturday.

Grammar practice

3 Complete the tables.

	✓	✗
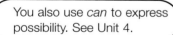	(I) I can swim.	(He) ....
	(We)	(They) They can't skate.
	(You)	(I) ....
	(He)	(We) ....

	?	✓/✗
	(she) Can she swim?	✓ Yes, she can.
	(you)	✗ ....
	(he) .... drive?	✓
	(they)	✓ Yes, they can.

Speak

4 Ask your partner the questions on the form in exercise 1. Then tell the class about your partner.

> **A** He/She can sing.

> **B** He/She can't tap dance.

Extra!

5 Write six sentences. Say what you can do and can't do.

I can cook.

Talk time

6a Listen and repeat the phrases. Then complete the dialogues.

1	of course	3	not really	5	Watch this
2	That's fine	4	You know		

1 **A** Can you swim?
  B Yes, ...of course... I can.

2 **A** Is that Cameron Diaz?
  B Cameron Diaz, who's she?
  A .... , the film star.

3 **A** Sorry, I haven't got a pen. Here's a pencil.
  B ....

4 **A** Can you tap dance?
  B You bet! ....

5 **A** Can you draw?
  B No, ...

6b Now listen and check.

ANIMALS QUIZ

7a Read and answer the questions.

1 Which bird can swim but can't fly?
a A duck.
b A chicken.
c A penguin.

2 How fast can a cheetah run?
a It can run at fifty kilometres an hour.
b It can run at a hundred kilometres an hour.
c It can run at a hundred and fifty kilometres an hour.

3 Where do armadillos live?
a They live in Africa.
b They live in Australia.
c They live in South America.

4 How far can a kangaroo jump?
a A kangaroo can jump nine metres.
b A kangaroo can jump six metres.
c A kangaroo can jump three metres.

5 Why do chameleons change colour?
a Because they are hungry.
b Because they are thirsty.
c Because they are frightened or angry.

6 Can a black widow spider kill you?
a Yes, it can.
b No, it can't.

7 A parrot can learn to speak.
What else can it do?

a Play the piano.
b Recognise colours and numbers.
c Read.

8 How long do elephants live?

a They live for seventy years or more.
b They live for fifty years.
c They live for thirty years.

9 How do ring-tailed lemurs fight?

a They dance.
b They make horrible smells.
c They bite.

10 Why do polar bears cover their noses?

a Because they don't want other animals to see them.
b Because they are cold.
c Because they are frightened.

7b **Now listen and check.**

Comprehension

8 **Complete the sentences with *can* or *can't*.**

1 Penguins ...can.............. swim.
2 Kangaroos .... jump nine metres.
3 Cheetahs .... run very fast.
4 A parrot can learn to speak, but it .... play the piano.
5 Other animals .... see a polar bear when it covers its nose.
6 Chameleons .... change colour.

Portfolio

9 Write a quiz about animals.
Go to page 133.

Listen and read

10 **Listen and read. Why is Laurie scared?**

Laurie	Drama lesson, Nick. Your favourite!
Mr King	Is everybody here? Right, let's start. OK. You're tired.
Sara	That's true!
Mr King	Come on, everyone. You're really tired... that's good. Now you're hot, terribly hot and you're thirsty.
Nick	Let's have a drink.
Mr King	Now it's late. You're cold. Brrrr! And you're hungry.
Mel	And a pizza.
Mr King	All right, calm down. Now you're frightened, you're really frightened.
Children	Ooooh! Aaah!
Mr King	OK. That's enough.
Laurie	Aaaagh!
Mr King	That's enough, Laurie.
Laurie	Look! There's a gigantic spider.
Mel	It's OK, Laurie. Don't panic. It's not a black widow spider!

Grammar focus

be + adjective

be	adjectives
I'm	hot, cold
You're	hungry
He's	thirsty
She's	right, wrong
It's	tired
We're	frightened
You're	angry
They're	bored

Which verbs do you use with these adjectives in your language?

Find and underline the adjectives in exercise 10.

Grammar practice

11 **Complete the sentences with the correct form of the verb *be* and an adjective.**

1 Calm down! Why .are. you .angry.........?
2 Washington DC is the capital of the United States. You're right........!
3 We don't want to go out, it's late. We ....
4 Can I have a drink? I ....
5 She wants a pizza. She ....
6 He doesn't like spiders. He .... of them.
7 No, five and eight aren't fourteen. You ....
8 Yuck! I can't drink this coffee. It ....
9 Open the window, I ....
10 Sonia wants to visit her friends. She ....

Pronunciation
/ð/ and /θ/

12a **Listen and repeat.**

/ð/	/θ/
that	thirsty
there	thanks
then	thing

12b **Write the words in the correct column.**

three   this   they   thirty

12c **Now listen and check.**

Speak

13 **Work with a partner. Give your partner an adjective to mime. Then change roles.**

A You're frightened.

Word Games

1 Tick (✔) the animals you can find in the picture.

- [ ] duck
- [ ] chicken
- [ ] penguin
- [ ] cheetah
- [ ] kangaroo
- [ ] spider
- [ ] parrot
- [ ] chameleon
- [ ] armadillo
- [ ] ring-tailed lemur
- [ ] polar bear
- [ ] elephant
- [ ] monkey

2 Write the missing letters in the boxes. What is the secret animal?

1 Brrr, $\boxed{\text{I}}$ 'm cold!

2 Polar bears and pen $\boxed{}$ uins like cold places.

3 No, I'm not h $\boxed{}$ ngry.

4 What $\boxed{}$ re you frightened of?

5 I'm $\boxed{}$ ot cold. I'm hot.

6 $\boxed{}$ re you tired? Yes, I am. Zzzzzz.

Culture spot

What do you like about Britain?

Read

1 Read what the people say about Britain.

The Roman baths in Bath

Robbie Williams
It's a free country.

Life in Britain is good because it's a free country. There are lots of things for young people to do. But I don't like the rain!

Luke Brown, 11
History fan

I like history. You can visit lots of museums and see things from Roman times in places like Bath. It's amazing! I think the best museums are in London. My sister and I sometimes go to London with my mum and dad. We have a great time!

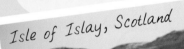

Isle of Islay, Scotland

Ross Carter, 10
No poisonous animals

I like lots of things about this country. But the best thing is there aren't any dangerous or poisonous animals. I like cats and I love dogs, but I'm frightened of snakes and big spiders!

Kylie Minogue
I enjoy the buzz.

I'm Australian but I love Britain. I enjoy the buzz of London and the beautiful countryside of Scotland.

Comprehension

2 Use the words from the chart to write six more sentences.

Ross doesn't like snakes.

Ross	likes	cats	London
Luke	doesn't like	dogs	the countryside in Scotland
Kylie		snakes	
Robbie		spiders	museums
		the rain	

Vocabulary

3 **Work with a partner. Can you guess the meaning of the words you don't know? Check with your teacher.**

It's a free country.

I enjoy the buzz of London.

You can see things from Roman times.

Speak

4 **Do a survey about your country.**

Write

5 **Write the results of the survey like this:**

Everybody likes the sunshine and the countryside.
Most students like the shops and the food.

What do you like about your country?

	everybody (100%)	most students (75%)	half of the students (50%)	some students (25%)	nobody (0%)
the weather					
the countryside					
the museums					
the shops					
the food					
the cars					
the pop music					

The letter

1 Listen and read.

1

Nick, the headteacher wants to see you, in his office, now.

Oh ... right.

You're in trouble, Nick.

2

I don't always pay attention, I often forget to do my homework, I sometimes bring my hamster to school ...

I'm often in trouble ...

and now I'm in serious trouble.

3

Hello, Nick. I've got a letter ...

Is it for my parents?

4

It's from the film company. You've got a second audition for the King Arthur film, in London, on Monday.

5

Well done, Nick. And good luck!

Thank you, sir.

2 Now answer the questions.

1 Who wants to see Nick?
2 Does Nick think he's in trouble?
3 What has the headteacher got?
4 What does the letter say?
5 Where is the audition?
6 When is the audition?

8 Places in town

1a Listen and write the number. 🎧

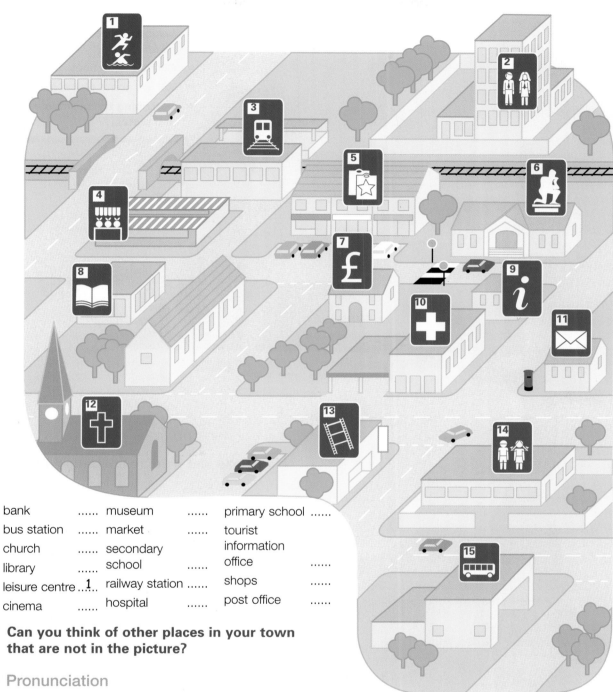

bank	...... museum	...... primary school ......
bus station	...... market	...... tourist
church	...... secondary	information
library	...... school	...... office ......
leisure centre ..**1**..	railway station	...... shops ......
cinema	...... hospital	...... post office ......

1b Can you think of other places in your town that are not in the picture?

🎧 Pronunciation

Stressed syllables

2 Listen and underline the syllables that are stressed. Which word is different from the other words?

1	library		6	market
2	primary school		7	leisure centre
3	cinema		8	bus station
4	hospital		9	railway station
5	post office		10	museum

3 Work with a partner. A says the name of a place and B finds the number of that place in the picture.

A The museum.

B Number 6.

Be quiet, please!

Castle Howard

- **Imperative: affirmative and negative**
- **Object pronouns:** *me, you, him, her, it, us, you, them*
- **Prepositions of place:** *in, on, opposite, near, next to, in front of, behind, between ... and ..., in the middle (of)*
- **Giving instructions**
- **Talking about places in a town**
- **Describing the position of objects and places**

Listen and read

1a **Read and write the missing words.**

Mrs Wilson	Be quiet, ..p̲l̲e̲a̲s̲e̲..! Nick and Laurie, sit down and be quiet! Now listen to me. Tomorrow (**1**)....................... is a class visit to Castle Howard.
Ricky	Where?
Mrs Wilson	Look at the map, Ricky. Castle Howard is near Malton. Take this (**2**)....................... home and give it to your (**3**)....................... . Sara, pay attention, please. Don't look out of the window. This is important! Come to (**4**)....................... at nine o'clock.
Laurie	Please, Mrs Wilson, do we ...?
Mrs Wilson	Just a minute, Laurie. Don't interrupt! Bring a jacket and a packed lunch. And what else?
Mel	A (**5**)....................... and a notebook?
Mrs Wilson	Yes, good! Put them in your (**6**)....................... tonight. Don't forget them. And, Nick, don't be late!

1b **Now listen and check.**

Comprehension

2 **Find a word in the dialogue for each of these things.**

1 letter...............

4 ....

2 ....

5 ....

3 ....

6 ....

7 ....

Grammar focus

The imperative	
Affirmative	**Negative**
Listen!	Don't interrupt!
Be quiet!	Don't be late!
Sit down!	

How do you say these sentences in your language?

Grammar practice

3 **Put the words in the correct order.**

1 `MAP` `AT` `LOOK` `THE`

 Look at the map.............................

2 `LATE` `BE` `DON'T`

3 `DOWN` `SIT` `PLEASE`

4 `INTERRUPT` `DON'T`

5 `LETTER` `THIS` `HOME` `TAKE`

6 `JACKET` `A` `BRING`

7 `FORGET` `DON'T` `PENCIL` `YOUR`

8 `ATTENTION` `PLEASE` `PAY`

Speak

4 **Work with a partner. Make imperative sentences using the words below.**

(don't)	listen	good	please!
	talk	attention	
	be	late	
	look	quiet	
	open	out of the window	
	close	the door	
	sit	your book	
	pay	the window	
	forget	down	
	bring	your pencil	

A Listen, please!

B Don't be late!

Grammar focus

Subject and object pronouns

Subject pronouns	Object pronouns
I	me
you	you
he	him
she	her
it	it
we	us
you	you
they	them

Look at the dialogue on page 96. What does *it* refer to in this sentence?

Give it to your parents.

Find another example of an object pronoun in the dialogue.

Grammar practice

5 **Complete the sentences with the correct object pronouns.**

1 My brother has a lot of homework.
   I sometimes help ....him..... .

2 Here's the letter. Take .... home.

3 Here are the books. Don't forget to take ....
   to the library.

4 Hello, Nick. This is Laurie. Can you call ....,
   please?

5 Penelope Cruz is his favourite star. He really likes
   ....

6 Hi, Ricky. It's Mel and Sara. We're at home. Come and
   see ....

7 Bye, Laurie. See .... later.

8 Ricky's cousins are here. Can we invite .... to
   the party?

Castle Howard

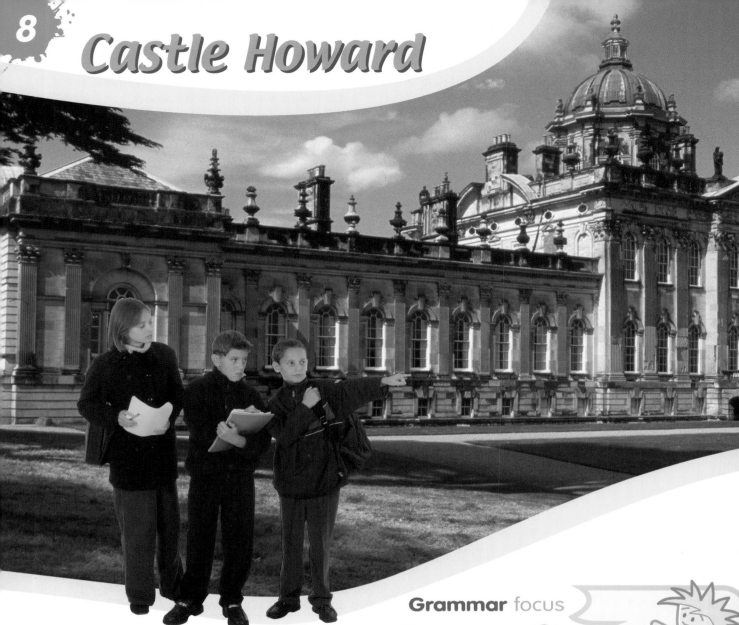

Listen and read

6 Listen to the class visiting Castle Howard. Use the words from the box to complete the dialogue.

| fountain | café | house | car | office | playground |

Mrs Wilson	Ready, everyone? Have you all got your worksheets? Right, read out the instructions.
Nick	Number 1. It's behind the ..house.... .
Mel	Number 2. They're between the house and the .... park.
Laurie	Number 3. It's next to the adventure ....
Sara	Number 4. It's in the middle of the ....
Ricky	Number 5. It's in front of the house, near the .... Be careful! Don't fall in!
Nick	Number 6. It's opposite the ticket ....

Grammar focus

Prepositions of place

in   in front of   on   behind

near   in the middle (of)   next to

opposite   between ... and ...

The statue and the fountain

Grammar practice

Complete the sentences with the correct prepositions.

in/on/next to

1 Nick's hamster is ....**in**........... his pocket.

2 His hamster is .... the book.

3 It's .... the desk.

opposite/in the middle of/behind/in front of

4 Laurie's bike is .... the café.

5 The café is .... the trees.

6 The trees are .... the park.

7 The park is .... the cinema.

near/between

8 Birmingham is .... Liverpool and London.

9 Manchester is .... Liverpool.

🎧 Talk time

8a Listen and repeat.

1 This is important.
2 Just a minute.
3 What else?
4 Right.
5 Be careful!

8b Complete the sentences with the correct phrases.

1 Ready everyone? .....**Right**,..... let's start.
2 Now listen carefully. ....
3 .... I'm not ready!
4 ....! There's an elephant behind you.
5 I've got my packed lunch, my pencil, my notebook. Now, ...?

8c Now listen and check.

8

🎧 **Read and listen**

9a **Look at the plan of Castle Howard. Complete the worksheet.**

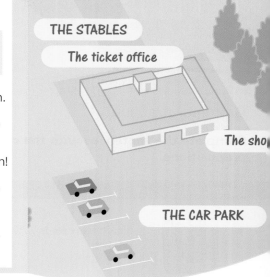

THE ADVENTURE PLAYGROUND

The statue

THE CAFÉ

THE FOUNTAIN

THE HOUSE

THE LAKE

THE STABLES

The ticket office

The shop

THE CAR PARK

Castle Howard Worksheet

Read the sentences and write the names of the places in the spaces.

The lake	The statue	The fountain
The café	The stables	The shop

1 It's behind the house.
   ...The fountain...............................

2 They're between the house and the car park.
   ....

3 It's next to the adventure playground.
   ....

4 It's in the middle of the fountain.
   ....

5 It's in front of the house, near the café. Be careful! Don't fall in!
   ....

6 It's opposite the ticket office.
   ....

9b **Now listen and check.**

Extra!

10 **Work with a partner. Look at the plan of Castle Howard. Ask and answer questions.**

A What's next to the car park?

B The shop.

A Is the adventure playground near the car park?

B No, it isn't.

Write

11a **Write five sentences about the map using the prepositions *in, next to, opposite, behind, in front of, near* and *between*.**

The fountain is behind the house..........

11b **Now write about the places in your town or city.**

My town is near Faro. It's a small town. There's a tourist information office in the square. Near the tourist office there's ....

Portfolio

12 **Write about your city. Go to page 134.**

Word Games

1 Read the text below and write where the people live.

There's a park behind my house.

My house is next to the post office.

I live opposite the post office.

We live between the shop and the church.

Our cat usually sits in front of our house.

Ryan ☐

Jenny ☐

Alana ☐

Tom ☐

Faisal ☐

2 Work out the code then write the names of the places.

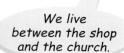

1 ◆ ♐ ❖ ♈ Ⅱ ⚹ ♐   ★ ♐ ⬇ ■ ⚹ ♐
  L e i s u r e   C e n t r e

2 ♈ ☉ ▢ ◆ ◆ ◆
  ....

3 ▢ ◆ ♈ ♐ ♋ ❖ ■ ➜ ◆
  ....

4 ☉ ❖ ⬇ ♐ ★ ➜
  ....

5 ★ Ⅱ ♈ ♐ Ⅱ ★
  ....

6 ★ ➜ ⚹ ▲ ♐ ■
  ....

3 Choose a sentence for each picture.

Bring a packed lunch.   Be quiet!
Don't fall in!   Put them in your bag.

1 Put them in your bag.

2 ....

3 ....

4 ....

Skills development

Days out

Read

1a Read the text and write the names of the places on the map.

1b What can you do in Manchester?

Manchester

5- to 10-year-olds

● For children, there's the Museum of Science and Industry. You can go on an old steam train called 'The Planet' to the world's oldest railway station!

The museum is in Liverpool Road.

11- to 16-year-olds ▶

● The Corner House is a big arts centre. On Saturday mornings, you can go to a club there. You can make videos, you can do photography and you can do computer art. There's a café on the first floor and there are three cinema screens.

The Corner House is in Oxford Road. It's just in front of Oxford Road Station. It's also between Deansgate Station and Piccadilly Station.

Adults ▼

● Adults can go on a tour of Granada TV Studios. The studios are next to the Museum of Science and Industry. They're in Water Street.

Or they can go to the City Art Gallery. It's near the Town Hall. There's a Tourist Information Office in the City Art Gallery.

For all the family ▼

Of course, you can all go to the Manchester United football ground and have a great day there.

2 Work with a partner. Can you guess what these words and phrases mean? Check with your teacher.

1 an old steam train
2 the world's oldest railway station
3 computer art
4 cinema screens
5 a tour
6 TV studios
7 an art gallery

A day out in and around London

The London Eye

Get a great view of London from the big wheel next to the Thames!

Chelsea Football Club

Come and see this famous football club.

The Bluebell Railway

Jump on and have a fantastic ride on the Bluebell Train!

The Bluebell Train

The Family Fun Club at the Barbican

Saturday morning cinema – just for children and young people.

The London Dungeon

Are you easily frightened? Then don't go to the London Dungeon. It's a museum about London life and history. But it's different. It's really frightening!

London Zoo

Come and see animals from all over the world. Don't forget your camera!

🎧 Listen

3 Read the information above and then listen to the interview. Find a place each person can visit.

1 <u>He can go to London Zoo.</u>

Write

4a Write a list of places to visit near your town or city.

For *5- to 10-year-olds*

1 ....
2 ....
3 ....

For *11- to 16-year-olds*

1 ....
2 ....
3 ....

4b Describe one of the places. What can you see and do there?

4c Write a publicity leaflet like the one above.

Speak

5 Describe a place to visit without giving the name. Your partner has to guess the name of the place.

A It's for children and adults. You can go swimming there. It's near the bus station.

B I know! It's the leisure centre.

8

Let's check ④

Vocabulary check

1 **Match the animals to the clues.**

chameleon	elephant	monkey	polar bear
cheetah	~~horse~~	parrot	spider
duck	kangaroo	penguin	

You can ride this animal. ....**horse**....

1 This bird can sometimes talk. ....
2 This black and white bird can't fly. ....
3 It's white and it lives in a very cold place. ....
4 It can change its colour. ....
5 It's grey and it's very big. ....
6 It can run very fast. ....
7 It lives in trees and likes bananas. ....
8 It lives in Australia and it jumps. ....
9 This bird can fly and swim. ....
10 It's very small but it can be frightening when it's in your room. ....

Write your score: .... /10

2 **Circle the correct word.**

We've got a Maths test today. I'm .**nervous**....... .
A thirsty   (**B** nervous)   **C** hot

1 I'm .... Can I have my lunch?
   A hungry   **B** wrong   **C** frightened

2 Kate is .... She wants a cola.
   A angry   **B** right   **C** thirsty

3 'Go to bed. It's very late.' 'But I'm not ....'
   A hot   **B** tired   **C** right

4 8 + 8 = 16. Yes. That's ....
   A wrong   **B** right   **C** bored

5 'I'm ....' 'Have a cold shower.'
   A frightened   **B** wrong   **C** hot

6 Rob's .... Where's his jacket?
   A cold   **B** thirsty   **C** hungry

7 I'm .... Let's go out.
   A tired   **B** bored   **C** right

8 Let's be quiet. The teacher is ....
   A hungry   **B** angry   **C** hot

9 9 + 9 = 17. No. That's ....
   A wrong   **B** right   **C** cold

10 'Help! There's a spider in the bath.'
   'Why are you ....? It isn't very big.'
   A frightened   **B** wrong   **C** tired

Write your score: .... /10

3 **Match the pictures to the words.**

a    b

c    d

e    f

g    h

i    j

k

	bank	....b......
1	bus station	....
2	café	....
3	hospital	....
4	library	....
5	market	....
6	museum	....
7	park	....
8	post office	....
9	railway station	....
10	shops	....

Write your score: .... /10

Grammar check

4 **Circle the correct imperative.**

Be / (Don't be) silly! This is important.

1 (Eat / Don't eat) sweets in class, please.
2 Please (speak / don't speak) English. I don't understand Russian.
3 Please (help / don't help) me. I can't do my homework.
4 (Stay / Don't stay) up late. We've got an important match tomorrow morning.
5 (Draw / Don't draw) on the desks. It's very silly.
6 Please (write / don't write) to us. We like letters and postcards.
7 (Read / Don't read) that book. It's very boring.
8 Please (invite / don't invite) Carl to your party. I really like him.
9 (Bite / Don't bite) me, you bad dog!
10 (Listen / Don't listen) to this CD. It's fantastic!

Write your score: .... /10

5 **Complete the sentences with an object pronoun.**

| me | him | ~~it~~ | her | them | us |

This is my letter. You can't read ....it......... .

1 He's wrong. Don't listen to ....
2 Sara's bored. Invite .... to your party.
3 Please help .... ! I can't swim.
4 Listen to .... We're right.
5 I've got some good video games. You can have .... this weekend.

Write your score: .... / 5

6 **Write sentences with *can* and *can't*.**

Penguins (fly / swim)
Penguins can't fly but they can swim...................

1 Parrots (swim / learn to speak)
....
2 Cheetahs (run very fast / fly)
....
3 Chameleons (dance / change colour)
....
4 Horses (fly / swim)
....
5 Spiders (bite / fly)
....

Write your score: .... /5

7 **Look at the map and use the correct words to complete the sentences.**

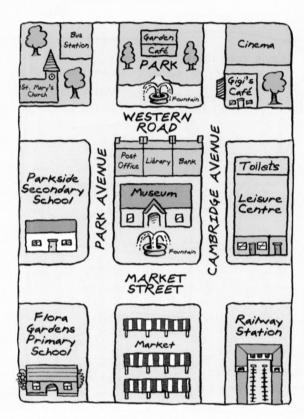

Gigi's Café is .next to. the cinema.
A behind   B opposite   C next to

1 The fountain is .... the park.
A behind   B in front of   C on
2 The post office is .... the library.
A opposite   B near   C next to
3 The library is .... the post office and the bank.
A in   B between   C in the middle of
4 The Garden Café is .... the park.
A in front of   B in the middle of   C between
5 The market is .... the museum.
A next to   B opposite   C in the middle of
6 The church is .... the bus station.
A near   B in   C opposite
7 The cinema is .... Cambridge Avenue.
A in   B near   C next to
8 The toilets are .... the leisure centre.
A opposite   B behind   C in front of
9 The primary school is near the ....
A cinema   B railway station   C market
10 The museum is opposite the ....
A bus station   B market   C cinema

Write your score: .... / 10

Write your total score: .... / 60

It's a Dog's Life!

1 **Listen and read.**

2 **Complete each sentence. Then write who says it.**

1 '........Get off......... the sofa.'
..Kevin and Charlie's dad......

2 '.................. silly, Charlie.' ....

3 'Here's the letter, Kevin. ....
it.' ....

4 'Sit here, Mutty. .... in.'
....

5 'Come on. .... up!'
....

6 '................. quiet, Charlie!' ....

9

Clothes

1 Listen and tick (✔) the clothes you wear to school. 🎧

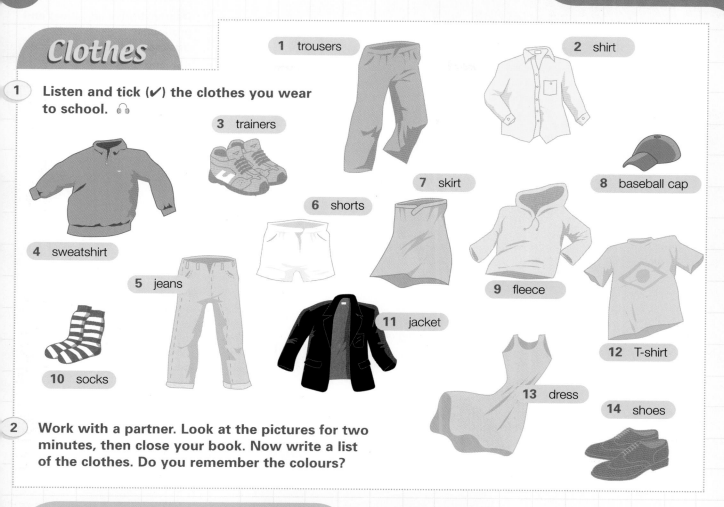

1 trousers
2 shirt
3 trainers
4 sweatshirt
5 jeans
6 shorts
7 skirt
8 baseball cap
9 fleece
10 socks
11 jacket
12 T-shirt
13 dress
14 shoes

2 Work with a partner. Look at the pictures for two minutes, then close your book. Now write a list of the clothes. Do you remember the colours?

Physical appearance

3a Listen and write the number of the person in the boxes. 🎧

☐ Rupal   ☐ Simon   ☐ Nicky   ☐ Ryan

Height	Eye colour
tall	blue
of medium height	brown
short	grey
Hair length	green
long	**Shades of**
medium length	**colour**
short	dark (brown)
Hair colour	light (brown)
brown	
black	
fair	
blonde	
red	
reddish-brown	
grey	
white	

a tall
long black hair
brown eyes

b quite tall
short fair hair
blue eyes

c medium height
very long
   blonde hair
blue-grey eyes

d quite short
medium-length
   reddish-brown hair
green eyes

3b Tick (✔) the words that describe your physical appearance.

What are you doing?

- Present continuous
- Demonstrative adjectives and pronouns:
  this/that, these/those
- *one* and *ones*
- Describing people and clothes
- Talking about present actions

Listen and read

1   **Listen to Nick getting ready for the audition.**

Mrs Mortimer	Nick! What are you doing up there?
Rachel	He isn't listening.
Mrs Mortimer	Nick! Are you doing your homework?
Nick	Yes!
Mrs Mortimer	No, you aren't. Why are you making all that noise?
Nick	I'm practising my dance routine.
Mrs Mortimer	What dance routine?
Nick	The one for the audition. It isn't going very well.
Mrs Mortimer	Well, come down now. It's time for lunch.
Rachel	Why are you wearing that silly hat? You look stupid.
Mrs Mortimer	Rachel! Stop it! You aren't eating, Nick. What's up?
Nick	Oh, I'm in a bad mood.
Rachel	Oh, poor thing! Are you having a bad day?
Nick	Yes, I am! I'm getting nervous about next Saturday.
Mrs Mortimer	It's only an audition, Nick. Don't worry about it.

Comprehension

2   **True (T) or false (F)? Correct the false sentences.**

1 Nick's at school.   ....F....
   <u>Nick isn't at school. He's at home.</u>

2 He's got homework to do.   ....

3 He's in a good mood.   ....

4 He's nervous about the audition.   ....

5 His audition is next Friday.   ....

Grammar focus

Present continuous

Affirmative	Negative
I'**m** listen**ing**.	I'**m not** listen**ing**.
You'**re** listen**ing**.	You'**re not** listen**ing**.
He/She/It'**s** listen**ing**.	He/She/It **isn't** listen**ing**.
We'**re** listen**ing**.	We **aren't** listen**ing**.
You'**re** listen**ing**.	You **aren't** listen**ing**.
They'**re** listen**ing**.	They **aren't** listen**ing**.

Questions	Short answers	
Am I listen**ing**?	Yes, I **am**.	No, I'**m not**.
Are you listen**ing**?	Yes, you **are**.	No, you **aren't**.
Is he/she/it listen**ing**?	Yes, he/she/it **is**.	No, he/she/it **isn't**.
Are we/you/ they listen**ing**?	Yes, we/you/ they **are**.	No, we/you/ they **aren't**.

Find examples of the Present continuous in the dialogue. Find two short answers.

How do you form the affirmative, negative and question form of the present continuous?

Grammar practice

3a **Complete the sentences with the affirmative forms.**

1 (wear) He*'s wearing* a blue shirt.
2 (do) I .... my homework.
3 (play) My friends .... football.
4 (go) We .... to the cinema.
5 (watch) She .... TV.
6 (read) They .... magazines.

3b **Write the sentences again in the negative form.**

He isn't wearing a blue shirt.

3c **Now write the sentences as questions.**

Is he wearing a blue shirt?

Pronunciation
/ŋ/

4 **Listen and repeat.**

1	doing	7	having
2	listening	8	getting
3	making	9	reading
4	practising	10	wearing
5	going	11	thing
6	eating	12	morning

Write

5 **Use the words to write two sentences.**

1 come down the ladder / go up
She *isn't coming down the ladder. She's going up*

2 cry / laugh
He ....
....

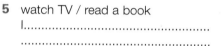

3 work on the computer / play games
They ....
....

4 do your homework / listen to CDs
You ....
....

5 watch TV / read a book
I ....
....

6 play rugby / play American football
We ....
....

Speak

6 **Ask and answer questions.**

A Is she coming down the ladder?

B No, she isn't.

Talk time

7a **Work with a partner. Complete the dialogues.**

1 A Come on, hurry up.
  B Why?
  A It's *time for* school.

2 A It's my birthday tomorrow and we've got an English test!
  B .... thing!

3 A Oh no! Oh, oh, dear!
  B What's .... ?
  A I haven't got my sports kit!

4 A What's the matter with you?
  B Oh, nothing. I'm just ....

5 A I'm really nervous about the football match tomorrow.
  B Don't .... it. It's .... a football match.

7b **Listen and check.**

 Extra!

7c **Use the phrases you completed in exercise 7a to write some dialogues. Then act them out.**

9

a a sweatshirt
b a T-shirt
c a jacket
d shorts
e trainers
f a skirt
g a skirt
h a dress
i socks
j jeans

Listen

8 Listen and circle the letters of the clothes that are mentioned.

What does *one* refer to?

the blue [jacket]   the blue [one]

What does *ones* refer to?

the grey [shorts]   the grey [ones]

Grammar focus

these, those

I like **these** trainers.

But I don't like **those** socks.

Grammar practice

9a Complete the sentences with *these* and *those*.

1 ..These.. are my trainers.
2 .... trainers are Angela's.

3 I love .... jeans.
4 I don't like .... trousers.

9b Complete the dialogue with *one* and *ones*.

A I like that jacket.

B The dark blue .one.?
No, I like the light blue .one. .

A Which shorts do you like, the long .... or the short ....?

B Oh, the long .... They're nice!

Speak

10 Work with a partner. Talk about the clothes you like in the picture. Use *these/those* and *one/ones*.

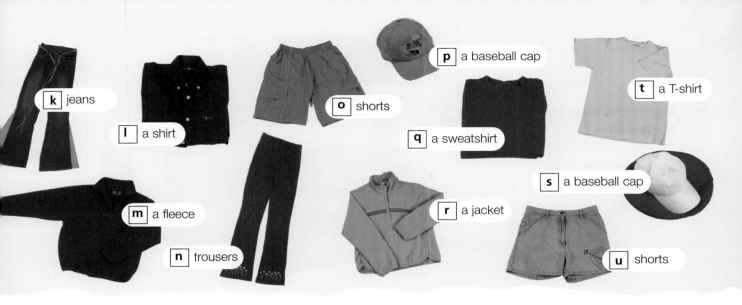

k jeans

l a shirt

m a fleece

n trousers

o shorts

p a baseball cap

q a sweatshirt

r a jacket

s a baseball cap

t a T-shirt

u shorts

Vocabulary

11 **Write the words in the correct column.**

- black
- blonde
- blue
- brown
- fair
- green
- grey
- medium length
- of medium height
- red
- reddish-brown
- short
- white
- (quite) tall
- (quite) long
- (quite) short
- dark (brown)
- light (brown)

Height	Hair length	Hair colour	Eye colour	Shades of colour
(quite) tall	(quite) long	black	blue	dark (brown)

Write and speak

12a **Describe the people.**

Lucy
She's quite tall. She's got long dark ....
brown hair and light blue eyes. ....

Lucy   Felix   Katie   James

12b **Work with a partner. Take turns to describe the people.**

> A She's quite tall. She's got long brown hair and blue eyes. She's wearing a yellow T-shirt.

Speak

13 **Play this game with a partner.**

A Who am I thinking of?
B Is it a man or a woman?
A It's a woman.
B Is she a film star, a sports star or a pop star?
A She's a pop star
B Has she got long brown hair?

Portfolio

14 **Design a catalogue page or describe a photo. Go to pages 134 and 135.**

9

🎧 Listen and read

15 **Listen and read. Nick is at his audition.**

In the waiting room

Mr Mortimer	How are you feeling, Nick?
Nick	Oh, OK.

The audition

Director	Hello, Nick.
Nick	Hello.
Director	Now, we're thinking of you for the character of Lancelot.
Nick	Oh. You mean … you aren't thinking of me for the character of Merlin?
Director	No, no. Lancelot is quite tall and strong, you see.
Assistant	How tall are you, Nick?
Nick	One metre 35.
Director	That's fine. Let's start. Now in this scene, Lancelot is talking to King Arthur. Can you read a little bit for us?
Nick	Yes, of course.

Comprehension

16 **Answer the questions.**

1 Where are Nick and his father?
   <u>They're in the waiting room.</u>
2 Why is he there?
3 Which character does Nick want to be?
4 Which character is Nick auditioning for?
5 How do you think Nick is feeling?

Extra!

17 **Describe one of the people in the photo. Your partner guesses who it is.**

18 **Work with a partner. Describe a person in your class. Your partner guesses who it is.**

A She's quite tall. She's got brown hair. She's wearing …

B That's Antonella.

Word Games

Match each speech bubble to a person in the picture.

Hello, Jenny. It's Paul here. Where are you? I'm sitting next to a tree, near the lake. **d**

My name's Jim. I'm wearing a baseball cap. My friend is called Tom. We're riding our scooters.

Hi, I'm Alex. I'm sitting near the ice cream kiosk. I'm wearing a big hat.

I'm called Ben. I'm wearing a red baseball cap and I'm skating.

I'm reading a book. My name's Sally.

I'm called David. I'm reading a magazine.

My name's Anna. I'm running and I'm listening to music.

I'm walking in the park with my friend Lizzie. We're eating ice creams. Lizzie's wearing a yellow T-shirt. My name's Julia.

My name's Rob. I'm playing football with my friend Mark. I'm not wearing jeans.

My name's Sonia. I'm playing with my little brother, Joe.

9

Culture spot

Our trip to London

Read

1 Before reading the text, tell your teacher what you know about London.

In this photo, we're riding on the London Eye. It's a big wheel, near the River Thames. The river runs through the centre of London.

I'm not frightened. Really!

Can I try your hat on?

This is Buckingham Palace. The Queen lives here. We're watching the Changing of the Guard. Alex is asking the soldier a question.

And this is St James's Park. It's near Buckingham Palace. Carla's writing a postcard. Alex and I are playing frisbee.

Comprehension

2 Read the text and find:

1 a place where you can buy presents
   The Apple Market in Covent Garden

2 the place where the Queen lives
   ....

3 a big clock
   ....

4 a river
   ....

5 a park
   ....

3 Write the names of the objects.

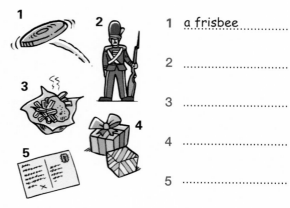

1 a frisbee ....

2 ....

3 ....

4 ....

5 ....

We're standing in front of Big Ben. It's a famous clock, next to the Houses of Parliament. Alex is being silly, as usual.

Here we are in the middle of Covent Garden. This is the Apple Market. We're buying presents to take home. Carla's eating fish and chips, yuk!

🎧 Listen and write

4a **Tick (✔) the places that are in London.**

☐ Tower Bridge
☐ The Empire State Building
☐ Trafalgar Square
☐ The Statue of Liberty
☐ Manhattan
☐ Oxford Street
☐ Madame Tussaud's

4b **Now listen and check. Write some information about each place.**

Tower Bridge: big, near the Tower of London

Vocabulary

5 **Work with a partner. Guess the meaning of the words you don't know. Then check with your teacher.**

Write

6 **Find some photos of a family trip and bring them to the class. Write a caption for each photo.**

Nick's news

1 Listen and read. 🎧

2 Now answer the questions.

1 What is Laurie doing?
   He's doing his homework.
2 What are Sara and Mel doing?
3 What is Ricky doing?
4 What is Nick's mum doing in picture 4?
5 What is Nick's news?
6 How do you think Nick is feeling today?

Food and drink

1 **Listen and read.** 🎧

What do you have for breakfast?

2 toast
3 orange juice
4 milk
5 jam
1 bread
7 butter
6 tea
8 yoghurt
10 cereal
12 eggs
9 pancakes
11 maple syrup
16 coffee
14 waffles
13 pastries
15 bacon

What do you have for a snack?

1 chocolate
2 crisps
3 peanuts
6 fizzy drinks
4 apple
5 sandwiches
7 milkshake
8 banana
9 biscuit
10 hamburger

What do you have in a sandwich?

1 cheese
2 ham
3 salami
4 chicken
5 tuna
8 mayonnaise
7 salad
6 tomatoes

2 **Ask and answer questions.**

A What do you have for breakfast?
What do you have for a snack?

B I often/sometimes/never have ....

I'm calling from the plane!

- Present simple and Present continuous
- Countable and uncountable nouns
- Talking on the phone
- Describing what you're doing
- Comparing what you usually do with what you're doing at the moment

Read

1 **Read and answer the questions.**

> **Ricky Gomez**   English homework
> ___
> What do you do in the summer holidays?
> I usually visit my family in New York. I go with my dad. We stay with my cousins.

> **Nick Mortimer**   English homework
> ___
> What do you do in the summer holidays?
> We don't go away in the summer. We sometimes go to the beach, for a day. And I go out on my bike a lot.

Listen and read

2 **Listen to the dialogue.**

Nick	Hello.
Ricky	Hi, is that Nick? It's Ricky here.
Nick	Ricky! Where are you?
Ricky	I'm flying over the Atlantic. I'm calling from the plane!
Nick	Oh, wow!
Ricky	Yeah, I'm playing video games, I'm drinking cola and I'm eating peanuts.
Nick	Lucky thing!
Ricky	And Dad's watching a film.
Captain	Ladies and gentlemen, I hope you're enjoying your flight. We're now flying at ...
Nick	I can't hear you. The line's breaking up. Call me from New York.
Ricky	OK, sure. Bye.

Comprehension

3 **Answer the questions.**

1 Who's Ricky calling?
   He's calling Nick.
2 Where's Ricky going?
3 What's Ricky doing?
4 Who's watching a film?
5 Why can't Nick hear Ricky?

1 What does Ricky do in the summer holidays?

   He usually goes ....

   ....

2 What do Nick and his family do in the summer holidays?

   They ....

   ....

3 What do you do in the summer holidays?

   ....

   ....

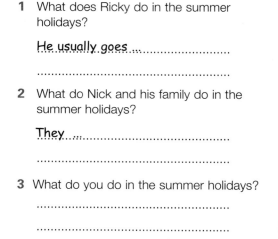

Grammar focus

Present simple and Present continuous

We use the Present simple to talk about habits and everyday routine.

I usually visit my family in the summer.

We use the Present continuous to describe what is happening at the time of speaking.

I'm calling from the plane.

Is it the same in your language?

Grammar practice

4 **Write PS (Present simple) or PC (Present continuous) next to each sentence.**

1 They often stay with their cousins. ...**P.S**......
2 What are you doing?
3 My dad's watching a film.
4 I sometimes go to the beach.
5 We don't go away in the summer.
6 He's eating peanuts.
7 I sometimes go out on my bike.
8 He's playing a computer game.

Speak

5 **Work with a partner. Talk about the people in the pictures.**

1 eat apple / every day

> She's eating an apple.
> She eats an apple every day.

2  play football / on Wednesdays after school

3  listen to the radio / before school

4  swim / every morning

5  watch TV / after school

6  read book / every week

Write

6 **Look at the picture. Write questions using the Present simple or the Present continuous.**

1 Where is Monica sitting?................................
   She's sitting on the bed.

2 Which football team does she like?............
   She likes Manchester United.

3 ....
   Peanuts? No, she isn't. She's eating crisps.

4 ....
   She plays tennis.

5 ....
   It's playing with the ball.

6 ....
   Yes, she goes skiing in the winter.

7 ....
   No, she isn't reading a book. She's reading a magazine.

8 ....
   No, she doesn't. It's very untidy.

9 ....
   She collects CDs.

10

🎧 Listen and read

7 Listen to the children making sandwiches.

Sara	What's in your sandwich, Laurie?
Laurie	Well, bread and butter.
Sara	Ha, ha, very funny. But what are you putting in the middle?
Laurie	Some ham and some cheese. What are you putting in your sandwich?
Sara	Some chicken and some bacon, I think.
Nick	What about you Mel?
Mel	I'm putting some cheese and some crisps in my sandwich.
Nick	Cheese and crisps! Oh, of course, you're vegetarian. I'm putting chicken, chocolate and salami in my sandwich.
Mel	Yuck!
Nick	Pass me a banana and some crisps. I can put them in, too. Lovely!
Mel	That's disgusting!

Comprehension

8 **What are they putting in the sandwiches? Write the person's initial under each picture.**

L = Laurie   S = Sara   M = Mel   N = Nick

L ....

....

Grammar focus

Countable and uncountable nouns

Countable nouns

Singular

Plural

Uncountable nouns

 an apple

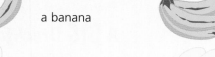 some apples

 bread/some bread

a banana

some bananas

 butter/some butter

 ....

....

 ....

 ....

 ....

....

 ....

 ....

 ....

 ....

 ....

....

Add the words from the box to the chart.

cereal	hamburger	biscuit	crisp
egg	milk	ham	orange juice

Complete the rule.

Remember: Use .*a*... or ...... with singular countable nouns. Use .... with plural countable nouns and with uncountable nouns.

Listen and read

9 **Listen to the dialogue.**

Ricky	Hi. It's Ricky here. I'm having breakfast, in New York.
Nick	Oh hi! What are you having?
Ricky	I'm having orange juice, and some pancakes with maple syrup and my dad's having eggs, waffles and coffee.
Nick	Mmm! Sounds great!
Ricky	Anyway, I'm just calling to say good luck with the film.
Nick	Thanks, Ricky! Have a great time! See you in September.

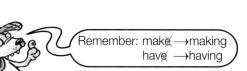

Remember: make →making
have →having

Comprehension

10 **Answer the questions.**

1 Who is Ricky calling? <u>He's calling Nick.</u>
2 Where is Ricky?
3 What's he doing?
4 How many kinds of food can you find in the dialogue?
5 How many kinds of drink can you find?

Pronunciation

/ʌ/ and /æ/

11a **Listen and repeat.**

/ʌ/	/æ/
butter	pancake
summer	sandwich
sometimes	hamburger
funny	apple
disgusting	ham
yuck	salad

11b **Work with a partner. Practise the words.**

10

🎧 Talk time

12a **Listen and repeat.**

1	Lucky thing!	**7**	Yuck!
2	Wow!	**8**	Lovely!
3	Is that (Nick)?	**9**	Disgusting!
4	It's (Ricky) here.	**10**	Mmm. Sounds great!
5	I can't hear you.	**11**	Have a great time!
6	What about you?	**12**	See you in September.

Di's Diner

A BIG Breakfast
cereal
2 eggs (any style)
bacon
pancake with maple syrup
waffle
yoghurt
bread and butter

12b **Put the sentences in the correct order. Work with a partner. Practise the phone conversation.**

> **A** Hi, is that Rosie?

> **B** Yes, who's that?

A	B
It's Alex here. I'm sitting on a beach in California.	Yes, see you! Have a great time!
Hi, is that Rosie?	Mmm. Sounds great.
Yuck! Disgusting!	No, it's lovely.
Oh, my mother's calling me. Enjoy your sandwich. See you in September. Bye!	Oh, I'm just having a peanut butter and banana sandwich.
What are you doing?	Yes, who's that?

Your favourite sandwiches

chicken salad sandwich
ham and cheese (toasted)
surf special: tuna with cheese
super salami

And to drink?
coffee
tea
orange juice
apple juice
milk
milkshake

 Extra!

13 **Work with a partner. Look at the menu. B is having breakfast at _Di's Diner_. A phones him/her.**

> **A** Hi! It's ... here. What are you doing?

> **B** Hi. I'm having breakfast. I'm having a/an/some ...

enjoy!
Have a nice day!

Speak and write

14 **Work with a partner. A is on holiday and calls B to find out what B is doing. Write the dialogue and practise it.**

Here are some ideas:

	Where are you?	What are you doing?
	in the park	playing football/volleyball/tennis/etc
I'm	on the beach	dancing
	at a party	making a sandwich
	at a disco	listening to music
	at a friend's house	watching a film/TV

Portfolio

15 **Find a recipe on the internet. Go to page 135.**

Sing a song
Dancing in the Moonlight
by Toploader

( )

Dancing in the moonlight
Everybody's feeling warm .... bright
It's such a fine and .... sight
Everybody's dancing in the moonlight.

(1)

We get it on most every night
When that moon is ..big.......... and bright
It's a supernatural delight
Everybody's .... in the moonlight.

( )

We like our .... and we never fight
You can't .... and stay uptight
It's a supernatural delight
Everybody's dancing in the moonlight.

( )

Everybody .... is out of sight
They don't bark and they .... bite
They keep things loose they keep it tight
Everybody's dancing in the moonlight.

1 Listen and put the verses of the song in the correct order. 🎧

2 Complete the sentences with the correct words.

and	dance	don't	here
~~big~~	dancing	fun	natural

3 Now sing the song.

Skills development

Families around the world

 Listen and read

1 **Listen and read.**

Sasha and Jack Delaney live in New York City, USA

Dad gets up at 6.30 a.m. and Mum goes to work at 7 o'clock. We have breakfast with Dad. We always have cereal, but Dad just drinks coffee. When we're at school, Dad does the shopping and the housework. Then he works on his computer. He's writing a book at the moment.

We have lunch at school. Dad always has a cheese sandwich for lunch – he loves cheese! When we get home from school, Dad usually helps us with our homework. He does the cooking, too. When Mum gets home from work, we all eat together.

Kaori Kino lives in Tokyo, Japan

My mother gets up at 6.30 a.m. She makes breakfast and packs my lunch for school. For breakfast we have cereal with milk and fruit. I like peaches with my cereal.

I take a packed lunch to school.

fried chicken

omelette

rice

pickled vegetables

sausages

salmon

pickled plum

Mum works in a shop. She usually has salad, fruit juice and coffee for lunch.

I do my homework when I get home from school … and I talk for hours and hours on the phone!

In the evening, we watch TV and I play the piano.

124

Luís da Silva lives in São Paulo, Brazil

We all get up at 7 a.m. For breakfast, I usually have bread and chocolate milk or fruit juice. My parents just have black coffee.

My mother and father both work. Mum cooks and cleans. Dad is a chauffeur.

I have lunch at school. I eat a lot of fruit. Mum and Dad have lunch at work. They usually have meat with vegetables.

In the evening, I do my homework and I play football with my brother. Mum often reads and Dad watches TV.

2a Write two lists. One list is for food you know. The other list is for food you don't know.

Words I know	Words I don't know
cereal	peaches

2b Compare your lists with your partner's lists. Ask your teacher about the words you don't know.

> Miss / Sir, what are 'peaches'?

2c On your lists tick (✓) the things that you like and cross (✗) the things that you don't like.

Write

3 Work in groups of three. Each person completes one part of the chart.

Speak

4 Ask questions and complete the rest of the chart.

> A What does Kaori / her mother have for breakfast?

> B What do they do in the evening?

5 Make a chart about your family. Use it to talk about your family's daily life.

Listen and write

6 Interview your teacher about his/her typical day. Now write a paragraph.

	Sasha and Jack / their father	Kaori / her mother	Luis / his parents
Breakfast	cereal		
Lunch			
Daytime activities			
Evening activities			

Let's check ⑤

Vocabulary check

① **Match the sentences (1–5) to the clothes (a–f).**

You usually wear white ones for tennis.   [d]
1 They can be long or short. Boys don't wear them. [   ]
2 They're often blue. Boys and girls wear them.   [   ]
3 You wear one when you're cold.   [   ]
4 You usually wear them with your trainers.   [   ]
5 You wear this when you play baseball.   [   ]

a baseball cap   d ~~shorts~~
b fleece   e skirts
c jeans   f socks

Write your score: …. /5

② **Write the words for the drinks.**

klim   ....milk.......
1 foceef   c...................
2 ate   t...................
3 gorane ceiuj o.................. j...................
4 kashkilem   m...................
5 zyzif krind   f.................. d...................

Write your score: …. / 5

③ **Put the words in the correct order. Then match the sentences to the people in the picture.**

hair / Mark / is / short / tall / got / and he's / black
Mark is tall and he's got short black hair.   b

1 short / Sabrina / she's / blue / and /eyes / is / got
....

2 tall / Emily / brown / is / hair / and / got long / she's
....

3 short / medium length / black hair / got / Steve / is / and he's
....

4 wearing / hair / Katy's got / and she's / a / baseball cap / long
....

5 tall / Richard is / black trousers / wearing / and he's
....

Write your score: …. /10

Grammar check

④ **Complete the sentences with the correct word(s).**

..These.. pancakes are really delicious.
(A These)   **B** This   **C** That

1 Can I have .... biscuit, please?
   A some   **B** a   **C** these

2 Do you like .... crisps?
   A this   **B** that   **C** those

3 Are you hungry? Have .... bread and cheese.
   A some   **B** a   **C** an

4 'Do you like Leila's jacket?' 'Do you mean ....?'
   A the blue ones **B** the blue one **C** the blue

5 I eat .... apple every day.
   A this   **B** a   **C** an

Write your score: …. / 5

⑤ **Write the sentences in the negative form.**

She is eating an egg sandwich.
She isn't eating an egg sandwich.
1 He is wearing my jeans.
....

2 I am getting nervous about the match.
....

3 We are talking about you.
....

4 They are making a noise.
....

5 You are drinking your milkshake.
....

Write your score: …. / 5

a   b   c   d   e   f

6 **Complete the sentences with the correct word(s).**

Dear Paul,

I'm on holiday in California with my sister, Sonia. We ...C... with my American friend, Scott Bryson. I (1) .... this postcard on Venice Beach. Sonia, Scott and two friends (2) .... volleyball and (3) .... them. (4) .... because it's very hot today and I'm a bit tired. So (5) .... an ice cream and writing to you. Sonia isn't very good at volleyball and she (6) .... very well!

I (7) .... Scott's family. His parents (8) .... really good cooks. His father (9) .... us delicious waffles with maple syrup for breakfast every day. And his mother (10) .... fantastic milkshakes. For dinner we (11) .... pizzas or hamburgers. It's great.

The Brysons (12) .... very near the sea. But it's OK because (13) .... a swimming pool in their garden. Sonia, Scott and I (14) .... our breakfast in the pool!

Some things in America are funny. They (15) .... 'sweets here'. They (16) .... 'candy'. And Scott's parents (17) .... to the shops. They (18) .... in their car.

(19) .... a good holiday? (20) .... hot in England? Write to me.

Love, Sophie xxx

	A	B	C
	A stay	B do stay	C are staying
1	A am writing	B writing	C write
2	A are playing	B is playing	C play
3	A I watch	B I'm watch	C I'm watching
4	A I don't play	B I'm not playing	C I'm not play
5	A I'm having	B I having	C I have
6	A isn't playing	B aren't playing	C not playing
7	A like	B liking	C likes
8	A be	B is	C are
9	A give	B gives	C is giving
10	A make	B makes	C is making
11	A usually having	B usually has	C usually have
12	A aren't living	B don't live	C doesn't live
13	A they've got	B they're having	C they got
14	A have sometimes	B sometimes have	C are sometimes having
15	A aren't saying	B say not	C don't say
16	A say	B saying	C are saying
17	A never walk	B walk never walking	C are never
18	A are going always	B always go	C go always
19	A You are having	B Are you having	C Have you got
20	A It is	B It's	C Is it

Write your score: .... / 20

7 **Match the answers (a–f) with the sentences (1–5). Then write out the answers in full using the Present simple or the Present continuous.**

Why is Steve dancing on the table?
[b] He's practising for his audition.

1 Why are you crying?
[ ] ....
....

2 She isn't eating her lunch.
[ ] ....
....

3 Look at Tina in this photo.
[ ] ....
....

4 My brother is working in Super Sports today.
[ ] ....
....

5 Lara's working on the computer.
[ ] ....
....

a) He (always / work) there on Saturdays.
b) He (practise) for his audition.
c) I (not / cry), I'm laughing.
d) She (always / do) her homework on it.
e) She (not / like) tuna.
f) She (wear) a silly hat.

Write your score: .... / 10

Write your total score: .... / 60

It's a Dog's Life!

1 Listen and read.

2 Read the story again and find:

- a sentence to say to a friend who is going on holiday.
- two sentences to write on a postcard to a friend.
- two sentences you say when you are surprised.

My Portfolio

What is the Portfolio?

It's a collection of documents about you. It helps show your skills in English. One section of the Portfolio is called the dossier.

What is in the dossier?

Each unit in this book has a project task which asks you to write in English about yourself and the world in which you live. Examples of these tasks are: write a profile of your favourite star, invent a quiz and design your ideal house. You can illustrate each task with drawings or photos. These projects form your dossier.

How do you create the dossier?

For each project, you need to do a draft. Your teacher will check your work and will give you advice. Then you can write the final version. You can include this in the dossier of your *Portfolio*.

Unit 1

1 Choose a topic.

1 Sports stars
2 Film stars
3 Bands

2 Work with other students who have chosen the same topic.

1 You can use the sentences in Unit 1, exercise 14.
2 Add additional information. Ask your teacher for help with the new words.
3 Illustrate the information with photos or drawings.

Sports stars

My favourite sports star is Michael
Schumacher.
He's German.
He's a Formula 1 driver.

Hi, I'm Michael Schumacher. I'm a racing driver.

Film stars

Name: Penelope Cruz.
Nationality: Spanish.
Date of birth: 28/04/1974.

I'm very famous!

Unit 2

1 Find information on the internet about a famous person and write about him/her.

Name: Prince William.
Date of birth: 21/06/1982.
Nationality: British.
Brothers and sisters: He's got a brother called Harry.
Pets: He's got a dog called Widgeon.

130

Unit 3

1 **Design your ideal house. Include the names of the rooms and the furniture.**

1 automatic drinks machine	6 mirror	11 swimming pool	16 lamp
2 computer	7 karting track	12 carpet	17 table
3 solar-powered heating	8 TV	13 water slide	18 notice board
4 basketball court	9 shower	14 posters	19 window
5 stereo	10 cupboard	15 chair	20 shelves

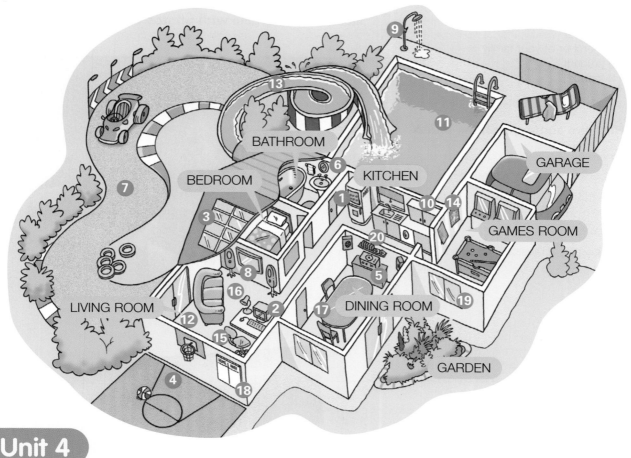

Unit 4

1 Use the internet to find out the birthday of a famous person. Write a birthday message like the one on page 55.

Happy Birthday!

Hi there, George.
So it's your birthday! How old
are you? That's so old! Never
mind, you're still my favourite.

Choose a project.

Project 1

1 **Choose a person to interview.**

- a teacher
- a member of your family
- a student
- a friend

2 **Here are some questions to ask.**

Where do you live?

What do you do in your free time?

Do you collect anything?

Which sports do you like?

Which sports do you play?

Do you play a musical instrument?

3 **Now write an article for a magazine. Illustrate the article with photos or drawings.**

Project 2

1 **Find information about a famous sports person. Write an article for a magazine like the one on page 68. Use these words to create questions.**

Who?

Where?

Which?

What?

Why?

Unit 6

1. Find information on the internet about your favourite star's typical day. Then write a paragraph.

2. Now write some questions to send in an e-mail.

   - Do you ever stay up really late?
   - Do you ever listen to music?
   - Where do you go at the weekend?
   - Are you ever impatient?
   - Are you ever bored? Why?

Cameron Diaz - Official Fan Club Site

New ▼ Send Receive Forward Delete

What do you do for fun, Cameron?

I shop, go horse riding, go to the beach and go out to eat. And I sometimes go to the gym.

Unit 7

1. Work in groups. Write a quiz about animals. Use a book about animals and a dictionary.

2. Exchange your quiz with another group's quiz. Answer their questions.

Where do kangaroos live?
Answer: They live in Australia.

How fast can lions run?
Answer: They can run at 80 kph.

Unit 8

1. Find your town or city on the internet. Write information about it.

2. Draw a map and write the names of places.

3. Use photos or drawings to illustrate the information.

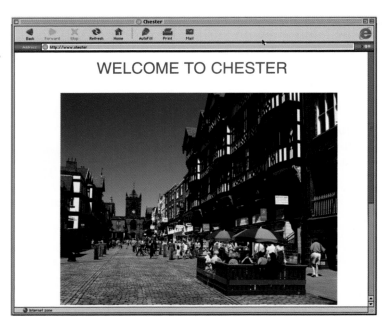

WELCOME TO CHESTER

Unit 9

Choose a project.

Project 1

1. Design a catalogue page. Find photos of people and describe what they are wearing.

a baseball cap

socks

trainers

trousers

a shirt

a skirt

jeans

a dress

shorts

a fleece

a jacket

a T-shirt

a sweatshirt

Project 2

1 **Describe a holiday photo.**

This is a photo of my sister, my mum,
my dad and me. We're in the sea,
but we aren't swimming. We're
walking in the water. In this photo
my mum's got medium-length blonde
hair but now she's got short red hair.

Unit 10

1 **Find a recipe on the internet. Type in 'recipes for children'. Here is one we found.**

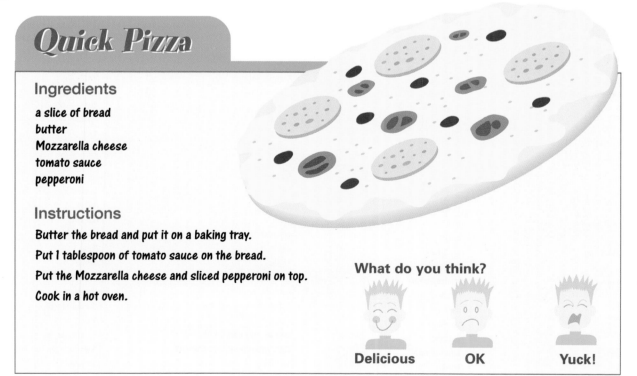

Quick Pizza

Ingredients

a slice of bread
butter
Mozzarella cheese
tomato sauce
pepperoni

Instructions

Butter the bread and put it on a baking tray.
Put 1 tablespoon of tomato sauce on the bread.
Put the Mozzarella cheese and sliced pepperoni on top.
Cook in a hot oven.

What do you think?

Delicious   OK   Yuck!

A

about	/əˈbaʊt/
about ▶ What about ...?	/ˈwɒt əbaʊt .../
activity centre	/ækˈtɪvɪtɪ sentə(r)/
acting	/ˈæktɪŋ/
address	/əˈdres/
adults	/ˈædʌlts/
adventure playground	/ədventʃə ˈpleɪɡraʊnd/
after	/ˈɑːftə(r)/
after-school activities	/ɑːftə skuːl ækˈtɪvɪtɪz/
after-school club	/ɑːftə ˈskuːl klʌb/
after that	/ɑːftə ˈðæt/
afternoon	/ɑːftəˈnuːn/
afterwards	/ˈɑːftəwədz/
age	/eɪdʒ/
all	/ɔːl/
all right	/ɔːl ˈraɪt/
allowed ▶ no dogs allowed	/nəʊ dɒɡz əˈlaʊd/
also	/ˈɔːlsəʊ/
always	/ˈɔːlweɪz/
amazing	/əˈmeɪzɪŋ/
American	/əˈmerɪkən/
and	/ənd, ænd/
angry	/ˈæŋɡrɪ/
animals	/ˈænɪməlz/
another	/əˈnʌðə(r)/
answer	/ˈɑːnsə(r)/
any	/ˈenɪ/
anyway	/ˈenɪweɪ/
apple	/ˈæpl/
April	/ˈeɪprəl/
archery	/ˈɑːtʃərɪ/
area	/ˈeərɪə/
Argentina	/ɑːdʒənˈtɪnə/
Argentinian	/ɑːdʒənˈtɪnɪən/
armadillo	/ɑːməˈdɪləʊ/
around	/əˈraʊnd/
arrive	/əˈraɪv/
Art	/ɑːt/
art gallery	/ˈɑːt ɡælərɪ/
arts centre	/ˈɑːts sentə(r)/
ask	/ɑːsk/
assembly	/əˈsemblɪ/
at five o'clock/at school	/æt, ət/
at last	/ət ˈlɑːst/
athletics	/æθˈletɪks/
attention ▶ Pay attention!	/peɪ əˈtenʃn/
audition	/ɔːˈdɪʃn/
August	/ˈɔːɡəst/
aunt	/ɑːnt/
Australian	/ɒsˈtreɪlɪən/

B

backwards	/ˈbækwədz/
bacon	/ˈbeɪkn/
bad	/bæd/
bag	/bæɡ/
bag ▶ school bag	/ˈskuːl bæɡ/
banana	/bəˈnɑːnə/
banana boat	/bəˈnɑːnə bəʊt/
band	/bænd/
bank	/bæŋk/
barbecue	/ˈbɑːbəkjuː/
baseball	/ˈbeɪsbɔːl/
baseball cap	/ˈbeɪsbɔːl kæp/
basketball	/ˈbɑːskɪtbɔːl/
bathroom	/ˈbɑːθruːm/
be	/biː/

Be careful!	/biːˈkeəfʊl/
Be quiet!	/biːˈkwaɪət/
beach	/biːtʃ/
because	/ˈbɪkʌz/
bed	/bed/
bedroom	/ˈbedruːm/
before	/brɪˈfɔː(r)/
begin	/brˈɡɪn/
behind	/brˈhaɪnd/
best	/best/
bet ▶ I bet ...;	/bet/ /aɪ ˈbet.../
bet ▶ You bet!	/juːˈbet/
between ... and ...	/brˈtwiːn ... ænd .../
big	/bɪɡ/
big wheel	/bɪɡ ˈwiːl/
bike	/baɪk/
bird	/bɜːd/
birthday	/ˈbɜːθdeɪ/
birthday cake	/ˈbɜːθdeɪ keɪk/
biscuit	/ˈbɪskɪt/
bite	/baɪt/
black	/blæk/
black coffee	/blæk ˈkɒfɪ/
black widow spider	/blæk wɪdəʊ/ ˈspaɪdə(r) /
blackboard	/ˈblækbɔːd/
blonde	/blɒnd/
blue	/bluː/
blue-grey	/bluːˈɡreɪ/
book	/bʊk/
bored, be bored	/bɔːd/
both	/bəʊθ/
boy	/bɔɪ/
bracelet	/ˈbreɪslət/
bread	/bred/
break	/breɪk/
break up	/breɪk ˈʌp/
breakfast	/ˈbrekfəst/
bridge	/ˈbrɪdʒ/
brilliant	/ˈbrɪlɪənt/
bring	/brɪŋ/
British	/ˈbrɪtɪʃ/
brother	/ˈbrʌðə(r)/
brown	/braʊn/
brush my teeth	/brʌʃ maɪ ˈtiːθ/
bulletin	/ˈbʊlətɪn/
bus, by bus	/bʌs/
bus station	/ˈbʌs steɪʃn/
but	/bʌt/
butter	/ˈbʌtə(r)/
buy	/baɪ/
Bye!	/baɪ/

C

café	/ˈkæfeɪ/
cage	/keɪdʒ/
cake	/keɪk/
calculator	/ˈkælkjʊleɪtə(r)/
call	/kɔːl/
called	/kɔːld/
Calm down!	/kɑːm ˈdaʊn/
camera	/ˈkæmrə/
camp fire	/ˈkæmp faɪə(r)/
can	/kæn/
can ▶ You can do it!	/juː kən ˈduː ɪt/
Can you repeat that please?	/ˈkæn juː rɪˈpiːt ðæt pliːz/
canoeing	/kəˈnuːɪŋ/
capital	/ˈkæpɪtl/
car, by car	/kɑː(r)/

car park	/ˈkɑː pɑːk/
carpet	/ˈkɑːpɪt/
cassette	/kəˈset/
cat	/kæt/
CD player	/siː ˈdiː pleɪjə(r)/
centre	/ˈsentə(r)/
cereal	/ˈsɪərɪəl/
chair	/tʃeə(r)/
chameleon	/kəˈmiːlɪən/
championship	/ˈtʃæmpɪənʃɪp/
change	/tʃeɪndʒ/
cheap	/tʃiːp/
Changing of the Guard	/tʃeɪndʒɪŋ əv ðə ˈɡɑːd/
character	/ˈkærɪktə(r)/
chauffeur	/ʃəʊˈfɜː(r)/
cheese	/tʃiːz/
cheetah	/ˈtʃiːtə/
chicken	/ˈtʃɪkɪn/
children	/ˈtʃɪldrən/
chocolate	/ˈtʃɒklət/
choose	/tʃuːz/
Christmas	/ˈkrɪsməs/
church	/tʃɜːtʃ/
cinema	/ˈsɪnəmə/
city	/ˈsɪtɪ/
class	/klɑːs/
class visit	/klɑːs ˈvɪzɪt/
classroom	/ˈklɑːsruːm/
clean	/kliːn/
clock	/klɒk/
close	/kləʊz/
clue	/kluː/
coffee	/ˈkɒfɪ/
cold, be cold	/kəʊld/
collect	/kəˈlekt/
colour	/ˈkʌlə(r)/
come down	/kʌm ˈdaʊn/
Come in/inside!	/kʌm ˈɪn, ɪnˈsaɪd/
Come on.	/kʌm ˈɒn/
come over. **Can you come over?**	/kʌm ˈəʊvə(r)/
company	/ˈkʌmpənɪ/
cook	/kʊk/
cooking, do the cooking	/ˈkʊkɪŋ/
corner	/ˈkɔːnə(r)/
corridor	/ˈkɒrɪdɔː(r)/
country	/ˈkʌntrɪ/
countryside	/ˈkʌntrɪsaɪd/
cousin	/ˈkʌzn/
cover	/ˈkʌvə(r)/
crisps	/krɪsps/
crossword	/ˈkrɒswɜːd/
cry	/kraɪ/
cup	/kʌp/
cupboard	/ˈkʌbəd/
cute	/kjuːt/
cycle	/ˈsaɪkl/
cycling	/ˈsaɪklɪŋ/

D

dad	/dæd/
daily activities	/deɪlɪ ækˈtɪvɪtɪz/
daily life	/deɪlɪ ˈlaɪf/
dalmatian	/dælˈmeɪʃn/
dance	/dɑːns/
dangerous	/ˈdeɪndʒərəs/
dark	/dɑːk/
date	/deɪt/
day	/deɪ/

days out	/deɪz ˈaʊt/
dear	/dɪə(r)/
December	/dɪˈsembə(r)/
delicious	/dɪˈlɪʃəs/
describe	/dɪsˈkraɪb/
desk	/desk/
dictionary	/ˈdɪkʃənrɪ/
different	/ˈdɪfrənt/
diner	/ˈdaɪnə(r)/
dining room	/ˈdaɪnɪŋ ruːm/
dinner	/ˈdɪnə(r)/
disco	/ˈdɪskəʊ/
disgusting	/dɪsˈɡʌstɪŋ/
do (gymnastics, athletics, homework)	/duː/
dog	/dɒɡ/
dollar	/ˈdɒlə(r)/
done ▶ **Well done!**	/wel ˈdʌn/
door	/dɔː(r)/
draw	/drɔː(r)/
drawers	/drɔːz/
dress	/dres/
drink	/drɪŋk/
drive	/draɪv/
DT (Design Technology)	/diː ˈtiː/
duck	/dʌk/
dungeon	/ˈdʌndʒən/
during	/ˈdʒʊərɪŋ/

E

each	/iːtʃ/
earring	/ˈɪərɪŋ/
easily	/ˈiːzɪlɪ/
Easter	/ˈiːstə(r)/
eat	/iːt/
Edinburgh	/ˈedɪnbrə/
egg	/eɡ/
Egyptian	/ɪˈdʒɪptʃən/
eight	/eɪt/
eighteen	/eɪˈtiːn/
eighteenth	/eɪˈtiːnθ/
eighth	/eɪtθ/
eighty	/ˈeɪtɪ/
elephant	/ˈeləfənt/
eleven	/ɪˈlevn/
eleventh	/ɪˈlevnθ/
else	/els/
else ▶ **What else?**	/wɒt ˈels/
England	/ˈɪŋɡlənd/
English	/ˈɪŋɡlɪʃ/
enjoy	/ɪnˈdʒɔɪ/
enough	/ɪˈnʌf/
e-pal	/ˈiː pæl/
especially	/ɪsˈpeʃəlɪ/
even	/ˈiːvn/
evening	/ˈiːvnɪŋ/
ever	/ˈevə(r)/
every	/ˈevrɪ/
everybody	/ˈevrɪbɒdɪ/
everyone	/ˈevrɪwʌn/
everything	/ˈevrɪθɪŋ/
Excuse me.	/ɪkˈskjuːz mɪ/
exercise book	/ˈeksəsaɪz bʊk/
expensive	/ɪkˈspensɪv/
eye	/aɪ/

F

fact ▶ **in fact**	/ɪn ˈfækt/
facts and figures	/fæks ən ˈfɪɡəz/

fair	/feə(r)/
fall (in)	/fɔːl ˈɪn/
family	/ˈfæmɪlɪ/
famous	/ˈfeɪməs/
fan	/fæn/
fantastic	/fænˈtæstɪk/
far (how far?)	/fɑː(r)/ /haʊ ˈfɑː(r)/
fast	/fɑːst/
father	/ˈfɑːðə(r)/
favourite	/ˈfeɪvrət/
February	/ˈfebrərɪ/
feel	/fiːl/
few	/fjuː/
fifteen	/fɪfˈtiːn/
fifteenth	/fɪfˈtiːnθ/
fifth	/fɪfθ/
fifty	/ˈfɪftɪ/
fight	/faɪt/
file	/faɪl/
fill in	/fɪl ˈɪn/
film	/fɪlm/
film star	/ˈfɪlm stɑː(r)/
find	/faɪnd/
Fine, thanks.	/faɪn ˈθæŋks/
finish	/ˈfɪnɪʃ/
first	/fɜːst/
first floor	/fɜːst ˈflɔː(r)/
fish and chips	/fɪʃ ən ˈtʃɪps/
five	/faɪv/
fizzy drink	/ˈfɪzɪ ˈdrɪŋk/
fleece	/fliːs/
flight	/faɪt/
Florence	/ˈflɒrəns/
fly	/flaɪ/
food	/fuːd/
football	/ˈfʊtbɔːl/
football club	/ˈfʊtbɔːl klʌb/
football ground	/ˈfʊtbɔːl graʊnd/
football match	/ˈfʊtbɔːl mætʃ/
football stickers	/ˈfʊtbɔːl stɪkəz/
footballer	/ˈfʊtbɔːlə(r)/
for	/fɔː(r), fə(r)/
forget	/fəˈget/
form	/fɔːm/
forty	/ˈfɔːtɪ/
fountain	/ˈfaʊntɪn/
four	/fɔː(r)/
fourteen	/fɔːˈtiːn/
fourteenth	/fɔːˈtiːnθ/
fourth	/fɔːθ/
France	/frɑːns/
free-time activities	/friː taɪm ækˈtɪvɪtɪz/
French	/frentʃ/
Friday	/ˈfraɪdeɪ/
fried chicken	/fraɪd ˈtʃɪkɪn/
friend	/frend/
frighten	/ˈfraɪtn/
frightened	/ˈfraɪtənd/
frisbee	/ˈfrɪzbiː/
from	/frɒm/
front ▶ in front of	/ɪn ˈfrʌnt əv/
fruit	/fruːt/
fun	/fʌn/
fun ▶ it's fun	/ɪts ˈfʌn/
funny	/ˈfʌnɪ/

G

games	/geɪmz/
garden	/ˈgɑːdn/
gentlemen	/ˈdʒentlmən/
Geography	/dʒɒˈɒgrəfɪ/
German	/ˈdʒɜːmən/
Germany	/ˈdʒɜːmənɪ/
get	/get/
get home	/get ˈhəʊm/
get nervous	/get ˈnɜːvəs/
Get off!	/get ˈɒf/
get up	/get ˈʌp/
gigantic	/dʒaɪˈgæntɪk/
girl	/gɜːl/
give	/gɪv/
go (swimming, skiing, cycling)	/gəʊ/
go away	/gəʊ əˈweɪ/
go for	/gəʊ fə(r)/
go out with friends	/gəʊ aʊt wɪð ˈfrendz/
go to (work, school, bed etc)	/gəʊ tə wɜːk, skuːl, bed/
go well	/gəʊ ˈwel/
goal	/gəʊl/
golf	/gɒlf/
good (at)	/gʊd/
Good afternoon.	/gʊd ɑːftəˈnuːn/
Good evening.	/gʊd ˈiːvnɪŋ/
Good idea!	/gʊd aɪˈdɪə/
Good luck!	/gʊd ˈlʌk/
Good morning.	/gʊd ˈmɔːnɪŋ/
Goodbye.	/gʊdˈbaɪ/
Goodnight.	/gʊdˈnaɪt/
grandad	/ˈgrændæd/
grandfather	/ˈgrænfɑːðə(r)/
grandma	/ˈgrænmɑː/
grandmother	/ˈgrænmʌðə(r)/
grandpa	/ˈgrænpɑː/
grandparents	/ˈgrænpeərənts/
grass	/grɑːs/
great	/greɪt/
Great Britain	/greɪt ˈbrɪtən/
Great!	/greɪt/
greek	/griːk/
green	/griːn/
grey	/greɪ/
gym	/dʒɪm/
gymnastics	/dʒɪmˈnæstɪks/

H

half (of)	/hɑːf/
half past one	/hɑːf pɑːst ˈwʌn/
ham	/hæm/
hamburger	/ˈhæmbɜːgə(r)/
hamster	/ˈhæmstə(r)/
hand	/hænd/
Happy birthday!	/hæpɪ ˈbɜːθdeɪ/
hat	/hæt/
Have a great time!	/hæv ə greɪt ˈtaɪm/
Have a nice day!	/hæv ə naɪs ˈdeɪ/
have a party	/hæv ə ˈpɑːtɪ/
have a shower	/hæv ə ˈʃaʊə(r)/
have breakfast/lunch/dinner	/hæv ˈbrekfəst, ˈlʌntʃ, ˈdɪnə(r)/
Have fun!	/hæv ˈfʌn/
have got, haven't got	/hæv gɒt, hævnt gɒt/
headteacher	/hedˈtiːtʃə(r)/
heating	/ˈhiːtɪŋ/
Hello.	/heˈləʊ/
help	/help/

here	/hɪə(r)/
Hey!	/heɪ/
Hi.	/haɪ/
hippo	/ˈhɪpəʊ/
History	/ˈhɪstrɪ/
hockey	/ˈhɒkɪ/
holiday, on holiday/in the holidays	/ˈhɒlɪdeɪ/
holidays ▶ in the holidays	/ɪn ðə ˈhɒlɪdeɪz/
home	/həʊm/
hope	/həʊp/
horrible	/ˈhɒrɪbl/
horse	/hɔːs/
horse riding	/hɔːs raɪdɪŋ/
hospital	/ˈhɒspɪtl/
hot	/hɒt/
hotel	/həʊˈtel/
hour	/ˈaʊə(r)/
house	/haʊs/
housework, do the housework	/ˈhaʊswɜːk/
How are you?	/haʊ ˈɑː juː/
How do you say ... in English?	/haʊ duː juː seɪ ... ɪn ˈɪŋglɪʃ/
How do you spell ... ?	/haʊ duː juː spel.../
how many?	/haʊ ˈmenɪ/
how old?	/haʊ ˈəʊld/
hundred	/ˈhʌndrəd/
hungry (be)	/ˈhʌŋgrɪ/
Hurry up!	/ˈhʌrɪ ˈʌp/

I

I can't hear you.	/aɪ kɑːnt ˈhɪə juː/
I don't understand.	/aɪ dəʊnt ʌndəˈstænd/
I'm fine, thanks.	/aɪm ˈfaɪn ˈθæŋks/
I'm sorry I can't (come to your party.)	/aɪm sɒrɪ aɪ kɑːnt ˈkʌm tə jɔː ˈpɑːtɪ/
ice cream	/aɪs ˈkriːm/
impatient	/ɪmˈpeɪʃənt/
in	/ɪn/
incredible	/ɪnˈkredɪbl/
indoor	/ɪnˈdɔː(r)/
industry	/ˈɪndəstrɪ/
insect	/ˈɪnsekt/
inside	/ɪnˈsaɪd/
instructions	/ɪnˈstrʌkʃnz/
interesting	/ˈɪntrəstɪŋ/
international	/ɪntəˈnæʃənl/
interrupt	/ɪntəˈrʌpt/
interview	/ˈɪntəvjuː/
into	/ˈɪntuː/
invite	/ɪnˈvaɪt/
Ireland	/ˈaɪələnd/
Irish	/ˈaɪrɪʃ/
Is that (Nick)?	/ɪz ðæt ˈnɪk/
IT (Information Technology)	/aɪ ˈtiː/ ɪnfəˈmeɪʃn tekˈnɒlədʒɪ/
It's two o'clock.	/ɪts tuː ə ˈklɒk/
It's (Ricky) here.	/ɪts ˈrɪkɪ hɪə(r)/
It's time for ...	/ɪts taɪm fə(r).../

J

jacket	/ˈdʒækɪt/
jam	/dʒæm/
January	/ˈdʒænjʊərɪ/
Japan	/dʒəˈpæn/
Japanese	/dʒæpəˈniːz/
jeans	/dʒiːnz/
jewellery	/ˈdʒʊəlrɪ/
Judo	/ˈdʒuːdəʊ/
July	/dʒəˈlaɪ/
jump	/dʒʌmp/
June	/dʒuːn/

Junior	/ˈdʒuːnɪə(r)/
just	/dʒʌst/
Just a minute.	/dʒʌst ə ˈmɪnɪt/

K

kangaroo	/kæŋgəˈruː/
karting	/ˈkɑːtɪŋ/
kill	/kɪl/
kilometre	/ˈkɪləmiːtə(r)/
kiosk	/ˈkɪɒsk/
kitchen	/ˈkɪtʃɪn/
know ▶ you know	/juː ˈnəʊ/

L

ladder	/ˈlædə(r)/
ladies	/ˈleɪdɪz/
lake	/leɪk/
lamp	/læmp/
language	/ˈlæŋgwɪdʒ/
late	/leɪt/
later that night	/leɪtə ðæt ˈnaɪt/
laugh	/lɑːf/
learn	/lɜːn/
leave	/liːv/
leisure centre	/ˈleʒə sentə(r)/
lessons	/ˈlesnz/
let	/let/
Let's (play).	/lets ˈpleɪ/
let's ▶ Well, let's see.	/wel lets ˈsiː/
letter	/ˈletə(r)/
library	/ˈlaɪbrərɪ/
life ▶ it's a dog's life	/ɪts ə ˈdɒgz laɪf/
light	/laɪt/
lights	/laɪts/
like	/laɪk/
line	/laɪn/
listen (to)	/ˈlɪsn tə/
listening test	/ˈlɪsnɪŋ test/
little	/ˈlɪtl/
little bit	/ˈlɪtl bɪt/
living room	/ˈlɪvɪŋ ruːm/
long (how long?)	/lɒŋ/ haʊ ˈlɒŋ/
Look at this!	/lʊk ət ˈðɪs/
look out of	/lʊk ˈaʊt əv/
lot ▶ a lot	/ə ˈlɒt/
lots of	/ˈlɒts əv/
love	/lʌv/
Lovely!	/ˈlʌvlɪ/
lucky, be lucky	/ˈlʌkɪ/
Lucky thing!	/ˈlʌkɪ ˈθɪŋ/
lunch	/lʌntʃ/

M

magazine	/mægəˈziːn/
main	/meɪn/
make (a noise)	/meɪk ə ˈnɔɪz/
man	/mæn/
mansion	/ˈmænʃən/
map	/mæp/
maple syrup	/meɪpl ˈsɪrəp/
March	/mɑːtʃ/
market	/ˈmɑːkɪt/
market garden	/ˈmɑːkɪt ˈgɑːdn/
mates	/meɪts/
Maths	/mæθs/
matter ▶ that doesn't matter	/ðæt dʌznt mætə(r)/
matter ▶ what's the matter?	/wɒts ðə ˈmætə(r)/
May	/meɪ/

mayonnaise	/ˌmeɪəˈneɪz/
me	/miː/
mean ▶ you mean …	/miːn/ /juː ˈmiːn/
mean ▶ What does … mean?	/wɒt dəz … ˈmiːn/
medium height (of)	/miːdiəm ˈhaɪt (əv)/
medium length	/miːdiəm ˈleŋθ/
metre	/miːtə(r)/
middle ▶ in the middle of	/ɪn ðə ˈmɪdl əv/
milk	/mɪlk/
milkshake	/ˈmɪlkʃeɪk/
minute	/ˈmɪnɪt/
mirror	/ˈmɪrə(r)/
Miss	/mɪs/
mobile phone	/məʊbaɪl ˈfəʊn/
moment	/ˈməʊmənt/
Monday	/ˈmʌndeɪ/
monkey	/ˈmʌŋkɪ/
months	/ˈmʌnθs/
mood ▶ in a bad mood	/ɪn ə bæd ˈmuːd/
more	/mɔː(r)/
morning	/ˈmɔːnɪŋ/
most	/məʊst/
mostly	/ˈməʊstlɪ/
mother	/ˈmʌðə(r)/
mountain	/ˈmaʊntɪn/
Mr	/ˈmɪstər/
Mrs	/ˈmɪsɪz/
Ms	/məz/
mum	/mʌm/
museum	/mjuːˈzɪəm/
Music	/ˈmjuːzɪk/

N

name	/neɪm/
nationality	/ˌnæʃəˈnælɪtɪ/
near	/nɪə(r)/
necklace	/ˈnekləs/
nervous	/ˈnɜːvəs/
never	/ˈnevə(r)/
Never mind.	/nevə maɪnd/
new	/njuː/
next	/nekst/
next (to)	/neks tə/
nice	/naɪs/
nine	/naɪn/
nineteen	/naɪnˈtiːn/
nineteenth	/naɪnˈtiːnθ/
ninety	/ˈnaɪntɪ/
ninth	/naɪnθ/
no	/nəʊ/
nobody	/ˈnəʊbɒdɪ/
noise	/nɔɪz/
noise ▶ make a noise	/meɪk ə ˈnɔɪz/
normal	/ˈnɔːml/
nose	/nəʊz/
not really	/nɒt ˈrɪəlɪ/
not very often	/nɒt verɪ ˈɒfn/
notebook	/ˈnəʊtbʊk/
nothing	/ˈnʌθɪŋ/
notice board	/ˈnəʊtɪs bɔːd/
November	/nəʊˈvembə(r)/
now	/naʊ/
number	/ˈnʌmbə(r)/

O

October	/ɒkˈtəʊbə(r)/
of	/ɒv, əv/
Of course.	/əv ˈkɔːs/

offer	/ˈɒfə(r)/
office	/ˈɒfɪs/
often	/ˈɒfən/
Oh dear!	/əʊ ˈdɪə(r)/
old ▶ so old	/əʊld/ /səʊ ˈəʊld/
oldest	/ˈəʊldɪst/
omelette	/ˈɒmlət/
on	/ɒn/
on holiday	/ɒn ˈhɒlɪdeɪ/
one	/wʌn/
one (this one, that one)	/wʌn/
only	/ˈəʊnlɪ/
open	/ˈəʊpən/
Open your books at page …	/əʊpən jɔː ˈbʊks ət peɪdʒ…/
opposite	/ˈɒpəzɪt/
or	/ɔː(r)/
orange	/ˈɒrɪndʒ/
orange juice	/ˈɒrɪndʒ juːs/
orchestra practice	/ˈɔːkɪstrə præktɪs/
other	/ˈʌðə(r)/
Ouch!	/aʊtʃ/
outdoor	/ˈaʊtdɔː(r)/
over there	/əʊvə ˈðeə(r)/

P

pack	/pæk/
packet of sweets	/pækɪt əv ˈswiːts/
Pakistan	/ˌpækɪsˈtɑːn/
palace	/ˈpæləs/
pancakes	/ˈpænkeɪks/
panic	/ˈpænɪk/
paper	/ˈpeɪpə(r)/
parents	/ˈpeərənts/
park	/pɑːk/
parrot	/ˈpærət/
part	/pɑːt/
partner	/ˈpɑːtnə(r)/
party	/ˈpɑːtɪ/
pass	/pɑːs/
pastry	/ˈpeɪstrɪ/
Pay attention!	/peɪ əˈtenʃn/
PE (Physical Education)	/piː ˈiː/ /fɪzɪkl edʒʊˈkeɪʃn/
peach	/piːtʃ/
peanut	/ˈpiːnʌt/
pen	/pen/
pence	/pens/
pencil	/ˈpensɪl/
pencil case	/ˈpensɪl keɪs/
penguin	/ˈpeŋgwɪn/
people	/ˈpiːpl/
perfect	/ˈpɜːfɪkt/
perhaps	/pəˈhæps/
period	/ˈpɪərɪəd/
person	/ˈpɜːsn/
pet	/pet/
photo	/ˈfəʊtəʊ/
physical appearance	/ˈfɪzɪkl əˈpɪərəns/
piano	/pɪˈænəʊ/
pickled	/ˈpɪkld/
picture	/ˈpɪktʃə(r)/
pink	/pɪŋk/
place	/pleɪs/
plane	/pleɪn/
planet	/ˈplænɪt/
platform	/ˈplætfɔːm/
play a CD	/pleɪ ə siː ˈdiː/
play football	/pleɪ ˈfʊtbɔːl/
play the guitar	/pleɪ ðə gɪˈtɑː(r)/

	/pli:z/	rugby	/ˈrʌgbɪ/
	/ˈpɒkɪt/	ruler	/ˈruːlə(r)/
ous	/ˈpɔɪzənəs/	run	/rʌn/
	/ˈpəʊlœnd/	run through	/rʌn ˈθruː/
ear	/ˈpəʊlə beə(r)/	Russia	/ˈrʌʃə/
	/ˈpəʊlɪʃ/	Russian	/ˈrʌʃn/
	/puːl/		
hing!	/pɔː ˈθɪŋ/	**S**	
usic	/ˈpɒp mjuːzɪk/		
al	/ˈpɔːtʃugɒl/	salad	/ˈsæləd/
uese	/ˈpɔːtʃʊgːz/	salami	/səˈlɑːmɪ/
fice	/ˈpəʊst ɒfɪs/	salmon	/ˈsæmən/
rd	/ˈpəʊstkɑːd/	same	/seɪm/
	/ˈpəʊstə(r)/	sandwich	/ˈsænwɪtʃ/
e (n)	/ˈpræktɪs/	Saturday	/ˈsætədeɪ/
e	/ˈpræktɪs/	sausage	/ˈsɒsɪdʒ/
	/ˈpreznt/	say	/seɪ/
nt	/ˈprezɪdənt/	scary	/ˈskeərɪ/
school	/ˈpraɪmərɪ skuːl/	scene	/siːn/
ninister	/praɪm ˈmɪnɪstə(r)/	school	/skuːl/
ly	/ˈprɒbəblɪ/	school bag	/ˈskuːl bæg/
	/ˈprəʊfaɪl/	school subjects	/ˈskuːl sʌbdʒɪkts/
	/ˈpjuːpəl/	school things	/ˈskuːl θɪŋz/
	/ˈpɜːpl/	school year	/ˈskuːl ˈjɪə(r)/
	/pʊt/	Science	/ˈsaɪəns/
ur hand up.	/pʊt jɔː ˈhænd ʌp/	scooter	/ˈskuːtə(r)/
		Scotland	/ˈskɒtlənd/
		screen	/skriːn/
iking	/ˈkwɒd baɪkɪŋ/	seaside (at the)	/ˈsiːsaɪd/
past two	/ˈkwɔːtə pɑːst ˈtuː/	second	/ˈsekənd/
to two	/ˈkwɔːtə tə ˈtuː/	secondary school	/ˈsekəndrɪ skuːl/
	/kwiːn/	secret ▶ the secret's out	/ðə siːkrəts ˈaʊt/
nnaire	/ˈkwestʃəˈneə(r)/	see	/siː/
	/ˈkwaɪət/	see ▶ you see	/siː/ /juː ˈsiː/
	/kwaɪt/	See you in September.	/siː juː ɪn sepˈtembə(r)/
	/kwɪz/	See you later.	/siː juː ˈleɪtə(r)/
		See you tomorrow.	/siː juː təˈmɒrəʊ/
	/ˈreɪdɪəʊ/	September	/sepˈtembə(r)/
e fridge	/reɪd ðə ˈfrɪdʒ/	serious	/ˈsɪərɪəs/
station	/ˈreɪlweɪ steɪʃn/	seven	/sevn/
	/riːd/	seventeen	/sevnˈtiːn/
ut	/riːd ˈaʊt/	seventeenth	/sevnˈtiːnθ/
	/ˈriːdɪŋ/	seventh	/sevnθ/
▶ Are you ready?	/ˈredɪ/ /ɑː juː ˈredɪ/	seventy	/ˈsevntɪ/
	/riːl/	share	/ʃeə(r)/
?	/ˈrɪəlɪ/	sharpener	/ˈʃɑːpnə(r)/
▶ She's really cute!	/ʃiːz rɪəlɪ ˈkjuːt/	shelf/shelves	/ʃelf, ʃelvz/
ise	/ˈrekəgnaɪz/	shirt	/ʃɜːt/
	/red/	shoes	/ʃuːz/
-brown	/redɪʃ ˈbraʊn/	shop	/ʃɒp/
tion	/redʒɪsˈtreɪʃn/	shopping	/ˈʃɒpɪŋ/
control	/rɪməʊt kənˈtrəʊl/	shops	/ʃɒps/
	/rɪˈpiːt/	short	/ʃɔːt/
	/raɪs/	shorts	/ʃɔːts/
	/raɪd/	shower	/ˈʃaʊə(r)/
us	/rɪˈdɪkjələs/	shower room	/ˈʃaʊə ruːm/
	/raɪt/	silly	/ˈsɪlɪ/
Am I right?	/raɪt/ /æm aɪ ˈraɪt/	sing	/sɪŋ/
	/rɪŋ/	sir	/sɜː(r)/
led lemur	/rɪŋ teɪld ˈliːmə(r)/	sister	/ˈsɪstə(r)/
	/ˈrɪvə(r)/	Sit down.	/sɪt ˈdaʊn/
ading	/ˈrəʊləbleɪdɪŋ/	six	/sɪks/
	/ˈrəʊmən/	sixteen	/sɪksˈtiːn/
times	/ˈrəʊmən taɪmz/	sixteenth	/sɪksˈtiːnθ/
	/ruːm/	sixth	/sɪksθ/
	/raʊnd/	sixty	/ˈsɪkstɪ/
	/ˈrʌbə(r)/	skate	/skeɪt/
		skateboard	/ˈskeɪtbɔːd/
		skateboarding	/ˈskeɪtbɔːdɪŋ/

ski	/skiː/	team	/tiːm/
ski (v)	/skiː/	teddy bear	/ˈtedɪ beə(r)/
skiing	/ˈskiːɪŋ/	teenager	/ˈtiːneɪdʒə(r)/
skirt	/skɜːt/	television (TV)	/teləˈvɪʒn/
small	/smɔːl/	ten	/ten/
smell	/smel/	tennis	/ˈtenɪs/
snack	/snæk/	tent	/tent/
snake	/sneɪk/	tenth	/tenθ/
so	/səʊ/	term	/tɜːm/
so (cute)	/səʊ ˈkjuːt/	terribly	/ˈterɪblɪ/
soccer	/ˈsɒkə(r)/	test	/test/
socks	/sɒks/	Thames	/temz/
solar-powered	/ˈsəʊlə paʊəd/	**Thank you./Thanks.**	/ˈθæŋk juː, θæŋks/
soldier	/ˈsəʊldʒə(r)/	**Thanks a lot.**	/θæŋks ə ˈlɒt/
some	/sʌm/	**Thanks anyway.**	/θæŋks ˈenɪweɪ/
something	/ˈsʌmθɪŋ/	**Thanks for your help.**	/θæŋks fə jə ˈhelp/
sometimes	/ˈsʌmtaɪmz/	**Thanks very much!**	/θæŋks verɪ ˈmʌtʃ/
song	/sɒŋ/	that	/ðæt/
Sorry I'm late.	/sɒrɪ aɪm ˈleɪt/	that's all	/ðæts ˈɔːl/
Sorry!	/sɒrɪ/	**That's easy.**	/ðæts ˈiːzɪ/
Sounds great!	/saʊndz ˈgreɪt/	**That's enough.**	/ðæts ɪˈnʌf/
south	/saʊθ/	**That's fine.**	/ðæts ˈfaɪn/
South America	/saʊθ əˈmerɪkə/	then	/ðen/
speak (French)	/spiːk/	there is/are	/ðeə(r)ˈɪz, ɑː(r)/
special	/ˈspeʃl/	these	/ðiːz/
spider	/ˈspaɪdə(r)/	things ▶ school things	/ˈskuːl θɪŋz/
sports	/spɔːts/	think (of)	/ˈθɪŋk əv/
sports star	/ˈspɔːts stɑː(r)/	third	/θɜːd/
stable	/ˈsteɪbl/	thirsty ▶ be thirsty	/ˈθɜːstɪ/
stand	/stænd/	thirteen	/θɜːˈtiːn/
start	/stɑːt/	thirteenth	/θɜːˈtiːnθ/
state	/steɪt/	thirtieth	/ˈθɜːtɪəθ/
statue	/ˈstætʃuː/	thirty	/ˈθɜːtɪ/
stay	/steɪ/	thirty-first	/θɜːtɪ ˈfɜːst/
stay in	/steɪ ˈɪn/	this	/ðɪs/
stay in bed	/steɪ ɪn ˈbed/	**This is important.**	/ðɪs ɪz ɪmˈpɔːtənt/
stay up late	/steɪ ʌp ˈleɪt/	those	/ðəʊz/
steam train	/ˈstiːm treɪn/	thousand	/ˈθaʊzənd/
stereo	/ˈsterɪəʊ/	three	/θriː/
Stop it!	/ˈstɒp ɪt/	Thursday	/ˈθɜːzdeɪ/
strictly no bikes	/strɪktlɪ nəʊ ˈbaɪks/	tidy	/ˈtaɪdɪ/
student	/ˈstjuːdənt/	time ▶ It's time for … / It's time to …	/ɪts ˈtaɪm fə, tə…/
stupid ▶ You look stupid!	/juː lʊk ˈstjuːpɪd/	**time ▶ What's the time?**	/wɒts ðə ˈtaɪm/
style	/staɪl/	tired	/ˈtaɪəd/
subjects ▶ school subjects	/ˈskuːl sʌbdʒɪkts/	to (Nick) from (Sara)	/tuː … from …/
summer	/ˈsʌmə(r)/	toast	/təʊst/
Sunday	/ˈsʌndeɪ/	toasted	/ˈtəʊstɪd/
sunshine	/ˈsʌnʃaɪn/	today	/təˈdeɪ/
sure	/ʃʊə(r), ʃɔː(r)/	together	/təˈgeðə(r)/
Sure, no problem.	/ʃɔː(r), nəʊ prɒbləm/	toilet	/ˈtɔɪlət/
surfing	/ˈsɜːfɪŋ/	tomato	/təˈmɑːtəʊ/
surname	/ˈsɜːneɪm/	tomorrow	/təˈmɒrəʊ/
surprise	/səˈpraɪz/	tonight	/təˈnaɪt/
Surprise, surprise!	/səˈpraɪz səˈpraɪz/	too (= also)	/tuː/
sweatshirt	/ˈswetʃɜːt/	too good to be true	/tuː gʊd tə biː ˈtruː/
swimming	/ˈswɪmɪŋ/	too much	/tuː ˈmʌtʃ/
		top	/tɒp/
T		tour	/tʊə(r), tɔː(r)/
table	/ˈteɪbl/	tourist information office	/ˈtʊərɪst ɪnfəˈmeɪʃn ɒfɪs/
table tennis	/ˈteɪbl tenɪs/	touch	/tʌtʃ/
take	/teɪk/	tournament	/ˈtɔːnəmənt/
take ▶ it takes an hour	/ɪt teɪks ən ˈaʊər/	tower	/ˈtaʊə(r)/
take the dog for a walk	/teɪk ðə ˈdɒg fər ə wɔːk/	town	/taʊn/
talk (on/about)	/tɔːk/	town hall	/taʊn ˈhɔːl/
tall	/tɔːl/	train	/treɪn/
tap dance	/ˈtæp dɑːns/	trainers	/ˈtreɪnəz/
tea	/tiː/	training	/ˈtreɪnɪŋ/
teacher	/ˈtiːtʃə(r)/	treasure hunt	/ˈtreʒə hʌnt/

tree	/tri:/	watch TV	/wɒtʃ ti: 'vi:/
tree house	/tri: haʊs/	wear	/weə(r)/
trip	/trɪp/	Wednesday	/wenzdeɪ/
trouble ▶ You're in trouble!	/jɔ:(r) ɪn 'trʌbl/	week	/wi:k/
trousers	/traʊzəz/	weekend ▶ at the weekend	/wi:k'end/
true	/tru:/	weird	/wɪəd/
try	/traɪ/	welcome ▶ You're welcome (to).	/jɔ: 'welkəm tə .../
T-shirt	/ti: ʃɜ:t/	Welsh	/welʃ/
Tuesday	/'tʃu:zdeɪ/	what	/wɒt/
tuna	/'tʃu:nə/	where	/weə(r)/
tutor group	/'tʃu:tə gru:p/	which	/wɪtʃ/
TV studios	/ti: 'vi: stʃu:dɪəʊz/	white	/waɪt/
twelfth	/twelfθ/	who	/hu:/
twelve	/twelv/	Whoops!	/wʊps/
twentieth	/'twentɪəθ/	whose	/hu:z/
twenty	/'twentɪ/	why	/waɪ/
twenty-eighth	/twentɪ 'eɪtθ/	wild animal	/waɪld 'ænɪməl/
twenty-fifth	/twentɪ 'fɪfθ/	window	/wɪndəʊ/
twenty-first	/twentɪ 'fɜ:st/	with	/wɪð/
twenty-five	/twentɪ 'faɪv/	without	/wɪð'aʊt/
twenty-four	/twentɪ 'fɔ:(r)/	woman, women	/wʊmən/ /'wɪmɪn/
twenty-fourth	/twentɪ 'fɔ:θ/	work	/wɜ:k/
twenty-nine	/twentɪ 'naɪn/	worksheet	/wɜ:kʃi:t/
twenty-ninth	/twentɪ 'naɪnθ/	world ▶ all over the world	/ɔ:l əʊvə ðə 'wɜ:ld/
twenty-one	/twentɪ 'wʌn/	worry	/wʌrɪ/
twenty-second	/twentɪ 'sekənd/	write	/raɪt/
twenty-seven	/twentɪ 'sevn/	wrong	/rɒŋ/
twenty-seventh	/twentɪ 'sevnθ/		
twenty-six	/twentɪ 'sɪks/	**Y**	
twenty-sixth	/twentɪ 'sɪksθ/	year	/'jɪə'r)/
twenty-third	/twentɪ 'θɜ:d/	year ▶ school year	/sku:l 'jɪə(r)/
twenty-three	/twentɪ 'θri:/	yellow	/jeləʊ/
twenty-two	/twentɪ 'tu:/	yes	/jes/
two	/tu:/	yoghurt	/jɒgət/
type	/taɪp/	young	/jʌŋ/
		Yuck!	/jʌk/
U		yummy	/jʌmɪ/
UK	/ju: 'keɪ/		
umbrella	/ʌm'brelə/	**Z**	
uncle	/'ʌŋkl/	zero	/'zɪərəʊ/
United Kingdom	/ju:naɪtɪd 'kɪŋdəm/	zoo	/zu:/
untidy	/ʌn'taɪdɪ/		
until	/ən'tɪl/		
up there	/ʌp 'ðeə(r)/		
up ▶ What's up?	/wɒts 'ʌp/		
Urdu	/'ʊədu:/		
USA	/ju: es 'eɪ/		
usual	/'ju:ʒʊəl/		
usually	/'ju:ʒʊəlɪ/		
V			
vegetables	/'vedʒtəblz/		
vegetarian	/vedʒə'teərɪən/		
very	/verɪ/		
view	/vju:/		
village	/'vɪlɪdʒ/		
visit	/'vɪzɪt/		
visitor	/'vɪzɪtə(r)/		
volleyball	/'vɒlɪbɔ:l/		
W			
waffles	/wɒflz/		
wait	/weɪt/		
Wales	/weɪlz/		
wall	/wɔ:l/		
want	/wɒnt/		
warm	/wɑ:m/		
Watch this.	/wɒtʃ 'ðɪs/		

Macmillan Education
Between Towns Road, Oxford, OX4 3PP
A division of Macmillan Publishers Limited
Companies and representatives throughout the world

ISBN 1 405 01902 6

First published 2005

Designed by Mackerel Limited.
Illustrated by Mark Davis.
Cover design by Mackerel Limited.
Cover photo by Alamy.

The authors and publishers would like to thank the following for permission to reproduce their material:

Blue Suede Shoes by Carl Lee Perkins © by Hi-Lo Music Inc – Public performance rights for USA and Canada controlled by Hi-LO Music Inc., a BMI affiliate. All other rights for the world controlled by Unichappell Music Inc (Rightsong Music Publisher) 1956, reprinted by permission of Carlin Music Corp., London, NW1 8BD. All Rights Reserved.
Dancing In The Moonlight Words and Music by Sherman Kelly © EMI Catologue Partnership, EMI U Catalogue Inc, EMI United Partnership Ltd and St. Nathanson Music Ltd, USA, Worldwide print rights controlled by Warner Bros. Publications Inc/IMP Ltd 1970, reprinted by permission of International Music Publications Ltd. All Rights Reserved.
Happy Birthday To You Words and Music by Patty S Hill and Mildred Hill © Summy Birchard Inc. USA, Keith Prowse Music Publishing Co Ltd, London, WC2H 0QY (for Europe) and Warner/Chappell Music Ltd, London, W6 8BS (for World excluding Europe) 1935, reprinted by permission of International Music Publications Ltd. All Rights Reserved.

Commissioned photography by Haddon Davies pp18/19, 20, 21, 22, 23, 28, 30, 36, 32, 42, 44, 45 (tl, bl), 50, 52, 54, 55, 56, 64, 66, 72, 76, 86, 94, 96, 108, 110/111, 112, 114/115 (kids), 116, 118 (boy), 120, 134 (b).

Research photography by ©Aardman/ W&G Ltd 1989 p10; John Birdsall Social Issues Photo Library p124 (l); reproduced courtesy of British Airways p114 (background); reproduced courtesy of Bluebell Railway Collection, Sheffield Park Station, East Sussex; Camera Press p130 (Prince William); Corbis p24 S.I.N. (b), pp24/133 (t) Frank Trapper (m – C Diaz), p57 Rufus F Folkks (Brad Pitt, J Lopez), p57 Siemoneit Ronald/Sygma (S M Gellar), p69 Bettmann, p92 Beirne Brendan (tl), p92 M Yamashita (bl, tr), p92 Roger Tidman (ml), p96, pp98/99 Adam Woolfitt, p103 Pawel Libera, p130 Sygma / Eric Robert (P Cruz), p131 Mitchell Gerber, p134 Richard Klune (t); Empics p24 (t), p57 (M Schumacher), p68, p130 (M Schumacher), p132 (b); Getty pp45 (br), 46, 49, 70 (bl), 78, 80, 103 (br), 115(not kids), p118 (not boy), p124 (tr, br), p125, p132 (t); Reproduced courtesy of IKEA Ltd (2003 catalogue); Image Bank p114 (Palace Guard), p133 (b), p135; The London Dungeon p103 (bl); ©News Flash, Scotland p48; © PGL Travel Ltd pp70/1; Pictures of Manchester p102; Taxi pp37, 64 (br); John Walmsley Education Photos pp18/9, 26.

Picture Research by Pippa McNee.

The publishers wish to thank the following: Alessia Batista, Danielle Batista, Gemma Bourne, Julie and Alastair Brett, Madeleine Brolly, Marie Collard, Darren Dimena, Philip Hathersall and all at The Dragon School, Oxford; Dan Fearn, Vicky Miller-Halliday, James Jones, Julie Jones, Alex Mylrea Lowndes, Benedict Smith, Elian Smith, Richard Stacey, Mrs Wingfield-Digby and all at Wychwood School Ltd, Oxford.

Printed and bound in Spain by Edelvives.
2009   2008   2007   2006   2005
10   9   8   7   6   5   4   3   2   1